Weight Loss Motivation & 100 Weight Loss Tips

The Ultimate MotivationGuide & 100 Weight Loss Tips

By Nicholas Bjorn

Book 1

Weight Loss Motivation

The Ultimate Motivation Guide

Weight Loss, Health, Fitness, and Nutrition

Lose Weight and Feel Great!

3rd Editon

By Nicholas Bjorn

or implied. Readers acknowledge that the author is not engaging in the rendering of legal, financial, medical, or professional advice.

Table of Contents

Introduction

I want to thank you and congratulate you for purchasing this book, "Weight Loss Motivation: The Ultimate Motivation Guide: Weight Loss, Health, Fitness, and Nutrition – Lose Weight and Feel Great!"

This book contains proven steps and strategies to keep your motivation up while implementing your weight loss plan.

Anyone can lose weight if they put their minds to it. Unfortunately, there are factors around you that may sabotage your mind. These factors affect your motivation and, ultimately, your performance. The tasks involved in losing weight become easier if you know how to stay motivated. This book discusses how motivation will improve your performance. It also discusses how the different types of motivation play a part in your success.

The book also explains how the different states of mind may affect our motivation. Sometimes, it is our own state of mind that hurts our chances of success. This book helps you deal with these mindsets to increase your chances of reaching your weight loss goals.

It is difficult to lose weight, and it is even more difficult to change your lifestyle and diet plan so that you can meet your goals. You may be overwhelmed and may want to give up immediately. This happens to everybody, and this book is here to help you stop feeling that way. It will provide you with tips to help you create a plan for yourself that is easy to follow. It will also provide you with tips you can use to push yourself to do better and meet your outcome goals!

Once you begin a diet, it does become difficult to stick to it, especially if you do not have a plan in place. This book will leave you with some tips you can use to stick to your diet and find ways to motivate yourself to do better.

Lastly, the book gives tips and strategies for you to overcome common weight loss challenges. It provides pragmatic ways for you to surely reach your goals. These tips and strategies apply to both men and women.

I have also included lots of inspirational and motivational quotes, designed to give you that extra boost in motivation that you might sometimes need. The methods suggested in this book are proven to keep you enthusiastic and hopeful. You should start reading today to begin your weight loss journey.

Be warned that there are no quick fixes in this book. I am not going to give you a diet to follow, and I am not going to give you any exercise routines – that is for you to determine by yourself or with the help of nutrition and fitness experts. My goal is to give you the motivation you need to keep on going and succeed in your personal journey toward health, fitness, and happiness, as well as a slimmer you.

You need to understand and accept the fact that you are bound to make mistakes. You may want a cheat day in the middle of the week or binge on something you crave. This happens because of restricting your diet, and this is something you should not do. Focus on choosing the right means to lose weight, and reward yourself when you achieve your goals. Do not berate yourself for making a mistake, but start where you stopped.

Thanks again for purchasing this book. I really hope you enjoy it!

FREE E-BOOKS SENT WEEKLY

Join North Star Readers Book Club
And Get Exclusive Access To The Latest Kindle Books in
Health, Fitness, Weight Loss and Much More...

TO GET YOU STARTED HERE IS YOUR FREE E-BOOK:

Visit to Sign Up Today!
www.northstarreaders.com/weight-loss-kick-start

Chapter 1: How Motivation Works

Finding a source for your motivation is essential if you want to get things done. The most difficult things in life require a lot of motivation to accomplish. With an ever-increasing number of distractions and opportunities to procrastinate around you, it is difficult to keep yourself motivated these days.

The challenge of motivation is most evident in matters concerning health. Given that most health-related tasks that need to be done have no immediate observable effects, you may easily lose motivation to do them. In working out for instance, many people lose interest when they can't see any visible results after a few sessions. This causes some impatient people to look for shortcuts. Some of the weight loss shortcuts found in the market, however, have dangerous effects on your health. To avoid these types of workout methods and to keep yourself motivated, you must understand how motivation works.

Phases of Motivation Needed to Get Things Done

There are three major parts of workout tasks where motivation is essential; before starting, in the middle of the task, and before ending the task.

It usually takes a lot of motivation to start a health-related task. The amount of motivation you need is greater if you hate the activity. This is the type of motivation needed when you are trying to convince yourself to get out of bed in the morning to start running.

Many factors affect your ability to start tasks. You may not be confident in your skills to accomplish a task, and you may be planning to learn more before jumping in. It could also be because of underlying fears that cause you to procrastinate.

A lot of motivation is also needed when you are in the middle of the task. You need motivation to remain focused on your goal until you accomplish it. This challenge is most difficult when the task requires a lot of time before it is done. You will need a lot of patience to keep yourself focused on the task at hand and to prevent your skeptical mind from sabotaging your success.

The last phase of motivation is usually needed for the final push to get a task done. This phase of motivation prevents you from taking too many breaks when you are almost at the finish line. People are vulnerable to procrastination when they are already near the end of their goals because they think that only a small amount of work is needed to get the task done.

For most types of tasks related to losing weight, you will need these three phases of motivation to reach your goal. You need a lot of motivation to get off the couch and work out every day. You will also need motivation to limit your calorie intake and avoid high-calorie food types. When you are already in the middle of a workout and diet program, it takes a lot of motivation for you to keep pushing to get better.

Motivation Suffers When You Hate the Activities

After working out and dieting for a while, beginners tend to form a negative attitude toward these tasks. They tend to hate the pain and the sweat, and this leads them to procrastinate on their scheduled workouts and fail on their meal plans when they are confronted with delicious types of food. They tend to hate waking up for a morning run or getting ready to go to the gym.

People cite a lot of reasons why they hate tasks related to losing weight, but you'll be surprised by how far off these are from the primary reason. The most basic source of all our hatred toward these tasks is fear. Your mind can become a victim of modern types of fear. These fears are the biggest factors that demotivate you even before you start.

In losing weight, one of the most common challenges is the fear of failing. If you have tried losing weight in the past and you failed at some point, you already have thoughts of failure ingrained in your mind. When you try to do the same task in the future, this lingering fear will remain in your mind. It will come out and do damage on your motivation when you are most vulnerable.

For most people, this is when they are in their beds, and they feel that they deserve to be resting. This is the time when you usually ask yourself: "What's the point?" You begin to question your whole motive for working out.

Given the strong effects of fear on you during this weak mental state, you need to learn how to control your own motivation. You need to be constantly aware of your level of motivation. As long as you do this, you will have the strength to carry on in your weight loss journey.

Learning about the Fear that Paralyzes You

Motivation is not just about pushing through against laziness. It is also about dealing with the fears you already have in your mind. Every time you are about to skip on a scheduled workout session or every time you place too much food on your plate, you should ask yourself these questions: Why am I doing this? What am I afraid of?

In the process of answering these questions, you will be able to reflect on your present attitude, and this will lead to keep working on your goal. By analyzing your thought process, you will not only prolong your motivation but also build a state of mind that allows you to control it.

As Zig Ziglar said, motivation is not permanent. Even if you succeed in boosting your motivation today, you will need to do it again tomorrow. That is the nature of motivation. You have to constantly work on it. You can do this by using both internal and external sources of motivation.

External and Internal Motivation

This process of self-reflection will help you develop strategies to help increase your external and internal motivation. External motivation is the type of motivation derived from sources outside of your mind. This is the type of motivation you experience when you feel like working out because you hear one of your favorite workout songs. The people and things that surround you affect your external motivation. Although this type of motivation is easy to create, it doesn't last very long. You should use it together with internal motivation.

Internal motivation happens when the principles and values you abide to become the reasons behind your actions. If you have this type of motivation, you do not need to hear any type of music just to start working out. Although this type of motivation is more difficult to develop, you should still work on it because its effects last longer. To have a strong source of internal motivation, you need a combination of two things: constant motivation practice and a set of positive principles to follow.

Surround Yourself with External Motivation

In the beginning of your weight loss program, it is understandable that your internal source of motivation may not yet be strong. In the early stages, you will need to make sure that the people and things around you motivate you to work harder. You should also decrease the factors that demotivate you in your surroundings. Tell your family and friends what you are doing so that they can encourage you to continue. Post a journal of your daily food and exercise regime on your Facebook page so that your friends can keep on pushing you to carry on. Only buy healthy foods; instead of heading for the cake section in the grocery store, head for the fruit section.

Developing Pro-Health Principles

Good health is a principle everybody should abide by. Unfortunately, many people take this aspect of their life for granted. It becomes a secondary priority next to finances and careers. If you want to lose your excess weight and keep that weight off, you need to develop a pro-health principle. This means that you want to lose weight because it is good for you. You are not working out and dieting just to look good, but you are doing so because of all the benefits that it brings to your life.

You will be able to develop this principle by constantly reminding yourself of the positive things that a healthy life can bring. For instance, by losing your excess weight, you will live longer, and you will have more time to enjoy with your family. If you love your job, losing weight and becoming healthier will allow you to increase your working hours on your projects. Keep focusing on your weight loss, and you will eventually develop this life principle.

Advantages of Focusing on Your Motivation

By learning how to focus and improve your motivation, you will learn a lot about yourself and how your mind works. You will not only learn about your fears but also where they come from and their particular effects on your behavior.

Motivation is a game changer. If you have tried and failed at losing weight in the past, learning about your motivation and practicing the principles offered in this book will significantly improve your chances of success.

By being aware of how motivation works, you will also develop a no-excuse mindset. Knowing that you can control your motivation prevents you from placing too much emphasis on uncontrollable factors in reaching your goals. You will hold yourself accountable in all your failures, and you would only have yourself to thank for all the successes that you gain.

Chapter 2: Diet Challenges that Make You Hate Losing Weight

Losing weight is not easy. There is a lot of muscle pain and sacrifice involved. If you haven't had any personal victories when it comes to losing weight, there are a lot of challenges that will make you lose motivation. You should be aware of these to prevent them from having too many paralyzing effects on your mind.

Fear

One of the biggest challenges is fear. You can try to avoid your fears, but doing so only strengthens them. The right way to deal with your fears is to identify and face them. Most modern fears are all in the mind. Many of them are not actually warning us from danger, as they should. Most of them only succeed in making us avoid new experiences. This is the nature of modern fears.

However, not all fears are bad. Some of them are rational. These types of fear warn you that your life may be in danger if you carry on with what you are doing. There are some types of fear, however, that have nothing to do with survival at all.

After identifying your fears, you need to separate the ones that are rational from those that are unnecessarily paralyzing you.

For most types of fear, the best way to deal with them is to constantly put yourself in experiences where you can face them. These experiences will desensitize you from the factors that you fear. As your mind becomes accustomed to working with these factors, it will no longer generate the sensation of fear every time you are about to face the same experience.

Paralyzing Self-Perception

Some types of fear also lead to a distorted way of seeing yourself. People who think of themselves as incapable of reaching their fitness goals sabotage themselves from reaching success. They surrender even before starting the battle.

For people who have this kind of self-perception, the first step is always to accept it. The usual reaction when someone points this out to them is denial. They tend to deny that their self-perception is the main factor that prevents them from even signing up to the gym or creating a diet plan. Accepting your self-perception is the first step to changing it.

After accepting this fact, the next step is to build your self-esteem by winning personal victories. Personal victories are the foundations of a healthy self esteem. You could start by taking on small weight loss-related tasks. When you achieve success with these tasks, you should write them down in a list. As the list of your personal victories become longer, you will become more confident to take on more difficult tasks.

How Others Look at You

For some people, their fear of being judged by others affects their actions too much. They fail to follow the plan in times when their mind becomes occupied by how other people think of them. People with this type of fear are prone to overeating when they are with a group of people who make fun of their attempt to lose weight.

The people around us can be mean. They ridicule people who are trying to lose weight because of their own failure to do so. They make other people feel horrible because deep inside, that's how they feel about their own weight and health problems. As you may have noticed, most fit people like talking about how they remain fit. This is not because they are self-centered but because many of them like to motivate others to do the same. A fit person feels bad every time they see someone they love suffering from weight issues.

You can deal with your fears, but you will not be able to change the negative attitude of others. However, you can control the people that you surround yourself with. If someone makes you feel bad for trying to lose weight or influences you to eat more than you should, avoid them at your time of weakness. In times when you are feeling down and your motivation is low, you should surround yourself with people who will lift your spirit and help boost your motivation.

Extreme Stress

If your mind is preoccupied with seemingly important thoughts and these thoughts cause you to become stressed out, you may not have the focus to continue on your workout and diet plan.

There are two approaches when dealing with these types of stress. You could deal with the cause of your stress first before continuing to work out, or you could try to stick to your plan even in the face of great mental stress.

In the beginning of your weight loss journey, you will have a hard time continuing on your weight loss plan when you are facing a great deal of stress. If this is true for you, you should do the first suggestion above. There are some types of people, however, who feel better when they work out. The good feeling that follows after working out helps in coping with the source of stress. If you are this type of person, you should do the second suggestion stated above.

You could schedule a session or two with a massage therapist to help relieve stress, or you could take up yoga and make it a part of your routine. Yoga not only helps you to get incredibly fit, but it can also help you clear your mind of the stresses and strains of each day.

Meditation is another great stress buster. It can teach you deep breathing techniques that you can do at any time and in any place. These techniques will help to eliminate any stress that you may be feeling. It can teach you to redirect your focus onto positive energies and banish the negative energy from your life. Meditation can be done for as little as five or ten minutes at a time, enough to help you feel refreshed like a new person and with your motivation levels fully intact.

Overthinking about Weight Loss

The mental toll of reaching your weight loss goal can also become a source of stress. When the stress caused by overthinking about weight loss becomes too high, it may also cause your motivation to work out to dwindle.

Success in weight loss can be achieved if you are doing the tasks needed to be done without spending too much time thinking about them. This is where mindfulness becomes useful. Mindfulness is a state of mind where you are only focused on one thing. The thing that you focus on should be the task at hand.

When it's time to work out for instance, you are only focused on that task and nothing else. It is inevitable for thoughts about your work or finances to creep into your mind. For very important thoughts, you need to have a piece of paper and write them down in a list. The less important thoughts, on the other hand, should be released. The idea is to get your focus back on the task at hand as soon as possible.

The Boredom Factor

The boredom factor is the single largest reason why people fall off their diets and lose the motivation to continue. It is all too easy to look at your diet sheet and see nothing more than a list of restrictive foods. Let's face it; there is only so much plain chicken or boiled fish you can eat, and who wants to eat green leafy vegetables all day long? Who wouldn't get bored with a diet sheet like that?

The answer to boredom and the best way to give your motivation levels a boost is to get creative with your food. Go to the store, and stock up on spices, herbs, fresh fruit and vegetables and then start looking for good ways to bring them into your meals. The following are just a few ways that you get creative with your food and really look forward to meal times:

- **Spice Things Up**

Spices and herbs are an excellent way to pep up your food. Instead of plain old chicken, add some fennel and rosemary. Rub mint into your next pork chop, and coat fish in lemon, mint, and pepper. If your food is bland, the spices and herbs will have a fantastic effect, giving them a completely different taste. So, don't be afraid to experiment.

- **Dress it Up**

A nice fruity vinaigrette is a great marinade for your meat or a lovely dressing for your vegetables – hot or cold ones. Try sprinkling a bit of raspberry vinaigrette over your broccoli or apple cider vinegar and pepper over your cabbage.

- **Infuse Your Olive Oil**

Instead of plain old olive oil, try infusing it with some of your favorite herbs and spices. Try adding a clove or two of garlic, a couple of sprigs of rosemary, or a few basil leaves to a bottle of oil. Red or green chili peppers or red pepper flakes do just as well, too. Leave the oil for a while to allow the flavor to infuse, and you'll find that it gives your food a real boost in flavor. Use it for sautéing or in your favorite healthy salad dressing to give it a bit of zing.

- **Soy Sauce**

This is especially true for the low-sodium kind. This makes a fantastic addition to any food. Sprinkle a few drops on your meat or over your vegetables. Add it to a healthy stir-fry or in with your rice as it's cooking. Soy sauce adds a little bit of extra flavor to anything, and there is little that it will not work with.

- **Make it Fruity**

Those dark green leafy vegetables that taste so bitter at times can taste wonderful with fruit. Serve up your spinach with raspberries, chunks of fresh pineapple, or segments of mandarin orange, and I guarantee you'll never shy away from a dark leafy vegetable again. Blend spinach or kale with fresh fruit to make a healthy and tasty smoothie, or dress it up with a fruity vinaigrette.

- **Make it Different**

Instead of serving up chunks of zucchini, spiral it instead, and use it as a healthy alternative to pasta. You can spiral carrots, cucumbers, any type of squash, or parsnips – you name it. You could sauté zucchini and carrots that have been spiraled and add a few olives, capers, and Italian tomatoes for a tasty Italian meal without the calories.

When you start to get bored with your food, instead of falling off the wagon and heading back to the cookies, simply change things up. Experimentation is the key here; see what works and what does not. Not only will you enjoy doing it, but you will also start to look forward to meal times again.

Aside from the mental aspects that prevent you from reaching your goals, you should also consider the external factors that may affect your motivation negatively. Here are some of them:

Presence of Food

You can't just rely on your willpower to avoid the temptations of food. Everybody has a breaking point when it comes to temptations. Your willpower should only be the last line of defense. You should actively decrease the amount of time that you are exposed to food while you are still developing the discipline to resist it. This means that you should choose the types of events that you go to socially. Avoid social events that encourage you to pig out.

There are some types of events, however, that are just too important to avoid. If you need to attend events like these and there are a lot of tempting foods in the venue, you should make sure to stay in areas that lessen your interaction with these foods. You should engage with people, for instance, to occupy your mind. Before you know it, the event is over, and you haven't taken a single bite.

There are also some food types that you just want to try because of taste. These are the types of food you want to try even if you are not hungry. In this case, you should not be afraid to take a small piece, and take just a few bites. The real challenge is not taking a second serving. You could use the "avoidance" strategy suggested above after you have taken your first bite.

Chapter 3: How to Boost Your Motivation to Maintain Your Diet Plan

We already touched on some parts of this topic in the last section of the previous chapter. In this chapter, we will discuss more strategies and scenarios where your motivation to avoid eating and lose weight will be put to the test.

Maintaining Your Diet

People usually eat more than their fair share when they haven't planned their food source for the day. Office workers are prone to this problem. They are usually absorbed in their jobs, and they don't give a lot of thought to the sources of their food. This makes them reliant on unhealthy food sources, such as preserved food products or fast food.

You can avoid these food sources by planning out your meals throughout the day. You will have a stronger chance of resisting food temptations if you are not hungry most of the time. To do this, you should evenly space your meals throughout the day.

The ideal meal plan is to eat 6 small meals in your waking hours. Most adults eat 3 big meals and countless snacks in between. After eating one of their big meals, they will probably feel hungry again after 2 hours. As it is not yet time for another big meal, they snack on the available food sources around them. For most people, the basis for their food choices is the taste. Tasty foods are usually high in fats and calories. You can avoid choosing these by creating a weekly meal plan.

Your Weekly Meal Plan

Before the week begins, you should plan the types of food that you will eat throughout the week. By doing this, you will be able to plan what to buy from the grocery store and adjust the number of calories you consume according to your fitness goals. A person living a sedentary lifestyle will need 1800 to 2600 calories per day. Women and older people generally need lower amounts.

To know how many calories to consume for you to lose weight, you should write down a list of foods that you eat daily for one week and calculate the corresponding number of calories that you consume each day. You could have a nutritionist do this for you if you are not sure how many calories each food type has. Alternatively, for detailed information on how calories work and how many daily calories you need, you can check out my book "Fitness Nutrition" https://www.amazon.com/dp/1514832968

It is easy to decrease the number of calories that you consume if you take away the unhealthy types of food from your diet. You should be aware of the food types that are high in calories. If you eat these types of food, you will eat too many calories before becoming full. Some of these food types are chocolate, cheese, sugar-filled drinks, nuts, and dried fruit. A handful of chocolates, for example, is equivalent to 2 cups of rice in calories.

Preparing Your Meals

Keep in mind that we are trying to avoid instances where you need to rely on preserved and fast foods in your meals and snacks. To do this, you will need to prepare your own food each day. It is highly suggested to prepare your food for the whole day every morning. You should follow the daily prescribed number of calories when preparing your meals. The next step is to divide the food that you prepare into six servings, and place them into vacuum-sealed containers to preserve their freshness.

The average person is awake for 16 hours a day. That means that you should eat your meals every 2 and a half to 3 hours. If you want to avoid eating before you sleep, you could modify the process by eating only 5 times a day. You will eat slightly bigger meals, but the number of calories that you consume will still be the same.

By following this plan, you will reduce the number of calories that you consume at one time. Your body will have more time to digest the foods that you consume, and by the time you eat your next meal, your body will have already digested the majority of the previous meal.

As your meals are evenly spaced, you will not become hungry in between meals. This will lessen your unhealthy snacking and prevent you from relying on fast foods and high-calorie packaged foods. You will be satisfied most the time, which means that you will have stronger willpower to resist offers of food.

How to Make People around You Help in Your Weight Loss Goals

Let People Know about Your Goal

You should tell the people around you about your plan to lose weight. Most people will understand and adjust their behavior towards you. If they know that you want to lose weight, they are less likely to offer you foods you are avoiding and support you in your food choices. This will also help them understand why you have a different meal schedule.

Document and Track Your Progress

If you let the people around you see your progress, it will help them understand your point of view. Creating a blog or posting your personal weight loss victories on your social media accounts is a great way to motivate you and keep you focused on your goals. Your friends who understand your goals will be supportive, further boosting your motivation.

Avoid People Who Sabotage Your Success

There are some types of people who will make fun of your effort. You should try to avoid insensitive people who will only make you feel bad. They usually undermine your effort and make you lose your motivation. They could also be the types of people who fill your head with negative thoughts. These are the people who constantly keep saying that you can't do it or that what you are doing is not important.

Hang Out with Supportive People

Surround yourself with people who share the same goals and concerns. You should find people who are also trying to lose weight. These are the types of people who congratulate you for your small victories and give you consoling words in the face of failure. They know how you feel because they are facing the same challenges. They will also be happy to have you around because your motivation also boosts theirs.

The following are tried and tested motivational strategies to help keep you on the weight loss track.

1. **Look for more than a single source of motivation**

If there is one way to keep you motivated on your weight loss journey, it's to find more than just one single reason to stay motivated. Some of the motivations that you could use to make sure you stick to a healthy diet are:

- You feel full of energy
- You jump out of bed in the mornings instead of pulling the duvet over your head
- You are at your ideal weight, and you want to stay there
- Your stomach is no longer bloated
- You enjoy food without suffering painful indigestion
- Your skin looks brighter and clearer

It's up to you to figure out what would motivate you to keep on eating those wholesome healthy foods and stay away from the bad stuff. Sit and think about it, make a list, and use that list as your means of motivating yourself.

2. **Set long-term goals**

Most people think only in the short term when it comes to losing weight, and many of their goals are unrealistic. The quickest way to lose motivation is to set a goal where you want to lose, say 10 lbs. in two weeks. First off, that is not a healthy way to lose weight and keep it off, and second, it is not really attainable, and when you see after week 1 that you've only lost 2 lbs., you'll realize that and your motivation is gone.

Long-term goals really are the difference between failing and succeeding. Weight loss itself is a short- or medium-term goal, but you need to look beyond that. Think about what you want to do when you get to your target weight. Maybe there is a particular activity you've always wanted to do but couldn't, maybe you want be able to run around after your children or your grandchildren, and maybe your goal is that you want to stay healthy and free of disease until your long healthy life comes to an end.

3. **Take it slow**

When you make the decision that you are going to lose weight and suddenly switch from doing little exercise and eating a poor diet to eating healthy and going into training, it can be something of a shock to your system. You will need to learn how to prepare food in a different way, how to eat more vegetables and fruits, and maybe even how to shop properly, and your body is going to react hard to a sudden change. It needs to learn how to digest these new foods and how to stop craving addictive foods for a start. The harder your body reacts, the more likely you are to give it all up, so the best thing to do is ease yourself in. Give your mind and body a chance to adjust to your new way of life, and you will be more likely to hang on to the motivation to succeed. Keep this in mind – it doesn't matter how fast you make changes; what matters is that you do, and you stick with them for the long term.

4. **Find treats and comfort foods that are healthy**

When you first make the change to a healthy diet, you might feel a little lost. The simple reason is that you are used to eating your favorite treats – those comfort foods are what you turned to in times of need, so you are feeling a bit empty, as if there's a big void that needs to be filled. There are plenty of healthy treats and comfort foods that can fill that void. If you have a sweet tooth and tend to turn to chocolate, simply puree up a banana and some cocoa powder with some ground flax to make a healthy chocolate pudding.

5. **Keep things simple**

You don't need to prepare complicated gourmet meals every day. Yes, it is nice to take time preparing a meal and making it look good, but for most meals, you can stick to basic foods like steamed vegetables and rice, a baked sweet potato, or a soup. Just use those herbs, spices, and vinaigrettes I talked about earlier to spice things up in simple ways. Find meals that you really enjoy, and just make a few simple changes to keep them interesting.

6. Never feel guilty

It takes time to make the transition from an unhealthy diet to a healthy one, and it is important that you do not get obsessive over what you are doing. Stress causes an awful lot of problems health-wise, and it is important that you do not stress yourself out over what you eat. Nobody can stick to a healthy diet every single day; we all have days where we give in to temptation. The important thing is that you don't feel guilty over it, and you don't use it as an excuse to slip back into old habits. Guilt is a negative emotion, and it simply makes you eat more to feel better about yourself. Don't punish yourself by eating less or exercising harder and longer because that won't work either. Simply take each day as it comes, and move on. If you slip up, simply pick yourself back up, and carry on with your new healthy diet.

7. Stay positive

Positive energy is the key to realizing your goals. Unfortunately, most people tend to focus so much energy on avoiding the bad stuff that they miss out on the fun of trying new foods and the effects that a good nourishing diet has on your body. Find healthy foods that you love to eat like fruits, some nuts, or a special healthy dinner. Eat them as often as you can so that you maintain a positive attitude, and keep that positive energy flowing through you.

Weight Loss Motivation Techniques – Will These Work for You?

Think tortoise and hare when you think of diets and losing weight – it really is slow and steady that wins. So, to keep you motivated and inspired to carry on, have a look at these common techniques for motivation, and ask yourself if they would work for you.

- **Sticking motivational quotes to your mirror**

Visual reminders are never a bad thing, so ask yourself if putting some motivational quotes on sticky notes on your mirror would help you. You can actually stick these notes anywhere – the fridge or in your car – just as little daily reminders about what you are trying to achieve.

- **Weight loss jars**

Visualization techniques are some of the best ways to keep yourself motivated. Get two jars – clear ones because you need to see what's inside them – and some colored pebbles or glass balls. Put one pebble or ball into one of the jars for every pound that you weigh, and for every pound you lose, take it out of that jar and put it in the other one. A quick glance is enough to tell you how well you are doing.

- **Food Labeling**

It's one thing to pack up your lunch and your snacks for the day, but what if you are tempted to eat it all in one sitting? Putting labels on the containers with the time you are meant to eat the food and how many calories are in the food can help you with portion control.

- **Leave your workout gear out and ready for use**

It can be difficult to walk past a mat that's been left unrolled without getting down to do a couple of crunches or a few yoga poses, but you could go one step further. Leave a set of hand dumbbells in your bedroom, perhaps a resistance band or an exercise ball in the lounge, and your running shoes by the front door as way of reminding you that exercise is important.

- **Buy some of your clothes in the next size down**

While it's always good to think about how you are going to lose the weight, it's also good to think about how you are going to look when you have lost it. So, prepare yourself for your weigh-in, and buy a few clothes that are the next size down. Hang them where you can see them when you wake up and when you go to sleep.

- **Pin a "fat" photo to your fridge**

Find the worst photograph of yourself, and pin it to your fridge door. This way, whenever you feel tempted and head to the fridge, it's the first thing you see. This should be motivation enough for you to leave the candy in the fridge and pick up an apple instead.

- **Share your food journal**

Everyone tells you that, when you are trying to lose weight, you should keep a journal of everything you eat. That's all well and good, but it doesn't stop you from failing. What you might do is opt to share your food journal with someone else. You can either email it to a close friend or family member who you know is going to support you, or you can go all out and publish it on your social media pages for all your friends to see.

- **Dress in your workout gear first thing every day**

Even if you are not intending to head out for a workout straight away, wearing the clothes is a great way of making sure that you will get out of that door and go for a run instead of finding an excuse not to.

- **Lolly sticks**

Write down all your fitness and diet goals on lolly sticks – for example, 25 crunches, walk 2 miles, etc. – and put them all in a plastic cup. Pull one out and complete it, and then put the lolly stick in another cup. Label the cups appropriately so you can see how much you have done and how much is left to do. As one cup begins to empty and the other starts to fill, you will find yourself even more motivated to keep going.

- **Always have food with you**

Diets do not have to be restrictive. In fact, those that are restrictive are the ones that you are more likely to give up on. Being on a diet isn't necessarily about cutting down on the amount you eat; it's about changing what you eat, and going hungry is not a good motivator. Always have food with you – a couple of bits of fruit, a tub of chopped up carrots, peppers and celery, or a low-fat yoghurt. This way, when you get the munchies, you will not be tempted to head for the bakery and pick up a double chocolate chip muffin with a side order of chocolate chip cookies. You will have food to eat – healthy snacks that will keep you full and satisfied – and keep the cravings at bay. Knowing that you are not about to go hungry and fall into temptation is motivation enough to keep going.

The Real Way to Get That Motivational Flow Going

- Don't choose to focus on positive or negative fantasies about your future self. Instead, focus on both. Doublethink everything, looking for the bad side as well as the good.

- Do train yourself to realize that, at some point, your willpower is going to disappear. Instead of wallowing in misery, tell people what your goals are, and ask for support to lower the chance of you failing

- Don't stick to picking a goal; pick all of the sub-goals as well. The goal is what you want to achieve, and the sub-goals are how you are going to achieve it.

- Look for the right role model. If you are scared of failing, then look for a role model who has failed. It is their story that will inspire you to succeed.

- Don't ever beat yourself up if you eat something that's not allowed. The power of regret is far more powerful if you use it before you do something or if you fail to do something than it is if you wait until afterwards.

- The most important thing is to realize that no motivational technique on earth is a magic pill. They can't make you lose weight – only you can do that and, if you don't really want to succeed, then you won't. If you do want to succeed, then you have taken the first step, and these motivational techniques will help you.

Chapter 4: How to Boost Your Motivation to Work Out

There are two major components of weight loss: your diet and your daily activities. To lose weight, you should eat just enough food to keep you energized for your daily activities. We discussed that in the previous chapter.

In this chapter, we will focus on building your motivation to keep exercising. Maintaining an active lifestyle will increase your metabolic rate. It will make your body burn more energy even while you are resting.

To be able to integrate workouts into your lifestyle, however, you should make sure that you enjoy them. If it feels too much like work, it will be too difficult to maintain. There will come a time that your mind will be defeated by the distractions and temptations around you.

How to Build Motivation for Working Out

Set Realistic Goals and Make a Plan to Reach Them

Before you can start lifting weights, jogging, or doing other types of activities, you should put in writing what you want to achieve. If you want to lose weight, you should set the exact number of pounds that you want to lose and the amount of time that you have to achieve your goal. You could also set your goals for specific body parts like your waistline or your arms.

Following the SMART philosophy for setting goals is an ideal tool to use. This ensures goals are specific, measurable, attainable, realistic, and have a timeline. You should then find a workout plan that fits your schedule and your personality. You should consider the time that you have for your workouts and the effort that you can devote to it.

Remind Yourself of the Benefits of Working Out

Being aware of the benefits of working out will help you continue doing it. You will also be able to build your willpower to avoid being lazy. This will remind you that you are not doing this just to look great but also to become healthier.

Make a List of Activities that You Enjoy

If you love dancing, you should include that into your workout plan. If you prefer sports, you should train for the type of sport that you want to participate in. By doing things that you like, you will be able to transition to an active lifestyle with much more ease.

Include a Variety of Activities in Your Workout Plan

Aside from doing what you love, you should also make it habit to try new things and to vary the activities in your workout plan. Lifting weights or running all the time will become boring after some time. If your body is not presented with a challenge every so often, it will no longer improve.

Prepare the Necessary Equipment and Outfits

Spending for your workout plan is like investing in your body; you will be expecting a return on your investment. Not only will you feel like an athlete, but this will also make you work harder and become more disciplined in following your strategies.

Make Your Workouts a Social Activity

You should avoid doing everything by yourself. Just like in your diet plan, you should also include the people around you. Join people who also like working out. Motivation, enthusiasm, and positive thinking are contagious. You will have a better chance of continuing your weight loss program if you have these people around.

Analyze the Factors that Motivate You

You should also use your metacognitive abilities to improve your performance. Every time you feel extra motivated, you should analyze the internal and external sources of your motivation.

Being aware of these factors will give you insight into how your mind works. You can use some of these factors to stimulate your motivation when you are feeling down.

Reward Yourself for Reaching Your Goals

Rewards are things that you allow yourself to have when you achieve a certain goal. They are expected to increase the likelihood that you will repeat your positive behaviors. You should decide on the rewards that you will give yourself when achieving your goals. The thought of the reward will help motivate you. In times when the workout routine becomes difficult, you should remind yourself of the reward that you will get if you push through.

You should make sure, however, that you will be able to follow through with your promise. The most important promises are the ones that you give to yourself.

Recharge Your Motivation to Exercise

The only thing that is standing between you and the body you want is mental block, so to get over those speed bumps and avoid the inevitable excuses, follow these top methods for rebooting your workout and your mental and emotional state.

You Think – My scales are stuck, why am I bothering?

Rethink – This pudge will go.

Stick with it. Weight loss is never consistent, and the scales, unless they are cheap or faulty, will never lie. First off, the more weight you have to lose, the quicker it will come off – IN THE BEGINNING. After that, it will all start to slow down. Most people reach a weight loss plateau, where they don't lose any weight for several weeks, and it is at this point that you must not give in.

One more important point – do not weigh yourself every day; it's a very bad habit. Your weight will go up and down daily, but it will go down overall. Weigh yourself once a week or fortnight. That way, any loss in weight is a much bigger motivator. Weighing yourself daily is the best way to demotivate yourself, so don't do it. Just because you aren't losing any pounds doesn't mean that your body isn't losing inches, and the only way to tell that is how your clothes fit. Give yourself plenty of credit for how much better you look, and use that as your motivation to continue.

Redo – Move your routine up a notch.

As you lose weight, your metabolism will adjust to accommodate the lighter, smaller you. That means you are going to have to change the way you encourage your body to burn fat and shed pounds. If you are already on a light diet of around 1500 calories a day, don't cut any more off. Instead, make your workouts more intense, and work out for a bit longer each time. Not only will this result in more calories being burned off, but it will also make your cardio capacity much larger. This means that you will find it easier to exercise and will be motivated to work out for just a little bit longer. Crank up the resistance on the stationary bike, set the treadmill at more of an incline, walk for a bit longer than you do now, walk at a faster pace, or go for one-minute interval runs. Between toning exercises, fit in a set of jumping jacks, running on the spot, or step-ups.

You Think – I really can't manage another rep.

Rethink – Don't my biceps look fantastic!

If you need a motivational boost or a bit of a lift, psych yourself up mentally and emotionally while you are training. This can increase your muscle power by up to 8%, as well as their size. Bigger muscles result in an increase in metabolism, which burns off fat faster. So, if you needed just one bit of motivation, there it is.

Mental imagery is a wonderful boost – when your arms or legs feel tired, imagine bigger and stronger muscles and tell yourself how great you look; you will get another rep or two out.

Redo – Take it down a notch.

If you really can't manage another rep at the same rate, lighten things off a bit. If you are lifting weights, knock the weights down by 10% until you know you can do another rep in good form. If you are sprinting circuits, slow it down for the last one. The more effort you put in, the better the rewards will be, so even if your final rep is at a lower rate than the previous ones, it's still more effort, and it will reap rewards. Don't ever beat yourself up if you can't do it, but keep this in mind: Pushing your limits a little further will get you results you never dreamed of seeing.

You Think – I can't run a mile!

Rethink – That jogger looks like Brad Pitt/Angelina Jolie – whoever takes your fancy at the time really!

When you are slogging your way through that mile, turn your thinking to what is going on around you. Yes, you may slow down a little, but you will keep on going, and you will finish that mile. Repeat a mental mantra over and over again – something like, "I am a running machine" – and you will find that you can go for longer and further.

Redo – Divide and conquer.

If you are running a mile, to start with, split it up into some running and some walking. Jog for maybe quarter of a mile, and the walk for a further half mile before jogging the final stretch. As you get better and fitter, as well as leaner, you can jog further and gradually cut down the walking time. If you can do this three times a week, it won't take long before you can run the entire mile. Your motivation? Your fitness and how you look. Think about how much better you feel, and you will keep on going. Do set up a routine for running, though. If you only go when you feel like it, it will not work.

You Think – I've damaged my knee/leg/arm, etc., so I won't be able to do any exercise for a month.

Rethink – Where did I put that Pilates DVD?

If you injure yourself and stop working out, it takes a maximum of three days for your body to start losing its conditioning. If that isn't enough motivation of you to get up and go, tell yourself this: There's more than one way to reach that goal. Start by making a list of all the negative thoughts you are having, and then turn them into positive thoughts. For example, "I can't go to my exercise class tonight; everything I've done will all go to waste," could be turned into, "Oh well, now I can start using that Pilates DVD I bought."

Redo – Switch things out.

Your regular exercise class might be out, but there are other options that are low or no impact. Depending on what injury you have sustained, a bit of moderate training on the elliptical bike can burn off up to 416 calories an hour, and water jogging can burn 512 calories an hour, as can cycling. These are all good alternatives but only if your injury allows it. If you can't exercise because your legs are injured or you have knee pain, you can still exercise the upper part of your body with hand weights. You can still sit on a chair and punch a boxing bag. Also, Pilates is a form of exercise that is gentle yet effective – designed to allow the maximum benefits in a safe way.

You Think – Spinning classes are way too intense for my liking.

Rethink – That guy over there in the Lycra shorts doesn't look as tough as he thinks.

We are afraid of the unknown – of what we don't know – so before you dismiss a particular exercise, have a go at it. You might just find that you enjoy it. Watch a class first, right from the start. If you see a spinning class from the middle onwards, the pace and the sweat are going to put you off, but if you see it from the beginning, you might just find that it is not that bad.

Redo – Find your own pace.

With most exercise classes, you are in control of how it makes you feel. Just because the rest of the class is throwing themselves about or the other runners on the track are sprinting all the way does not mean that you have to. If there comes a point in the class where the instructor tells you to increase resistance, only go as far as you are comfortable going. If you get tired and can't keep up, slow things down a bit. The idea of exercise is to get the hang of it while doing it correctly and safely and to have fun. Go into each class telling yourself that you are there to enjoy yourself, and you will.

You Think – I can only exercise at home; that's not going to work!

Rethink – There really is no place like home!

The first thing you have do is work out what is going to motivate you to get off the couch and stay off it. Then, you need to come up with a plan that is going to put you in the frame of mind to commit to exercising at home. Put your workout clothes on when you get home from work or first thing in the morning so that you get in the right mindset and know you are going to exercise. Create a schedule that has accountability in it. For example, get a friend to come around on certain days, and do those kickboxing or fitness DVDs.

Redo – Get a takeaway.

I don't mean the fast food one. If you can't afford to join a gym, you can have one beamed into you lounge for a fraction of the cost. Using email and website, personal trainers are there to help you without you having to leave your own home. Some of them will provide you with a customized routine to follow, as well as a diet plan.

You Think – I can't stay on that cardio machine for more than 30 minutes; it's like a form of slow torture!

Rethink – Who's going to be sent home tonight on BB/Jungle/X-Factor, etc.?

When you are on the treadmill, don't waste your time thinking about the exercise you are doing; it won't work. Instead, turn to other things, like watching your favorite TV program or plugging into your music and losing yourself in it. You might just be surprised at how fast the time goes and how much more you achieve when your mind is elsewhere.

Redo – Work first, rest later.

Plan your routine so that you start hard and fast and slow down towards the end. If you start off with high-intensity workouts and then go on down to lower intensity, especially on the treadmill, you will find that more fat is burned, and your workout won't feel quite so stressful. Your motivation is that you know you can finish light and not be absolutely worn out, dripping sweat, and feeling like you couldn't move another step if you wanted to. Try this 45-minute plan – warm up for 5 minutes at a nice, easy pace. Increase speed up to a moderate level, and for 20 minutes, increase your speed or incline by 1% every 2 minutes. Then, lower the incline and/or the speed slightly for 15 minutes, followed by 5 minutes at a nice, easy cool-down pace.

You Think – I haven't got the energy to exercise after work.

Rethink – Just 10 minutes, that's all!

There is a huge difference between mental and physical tiredness. Believe it or not, physical activity can knock down your mental fatigue. Tell yourself that you will do just 10 minutes, and you will find, more often than not, that you end up doing more, simply because once you get going, your tiredness and fatigue disappears. Not only that, but your mood improves, too.

Redo – Stack it in your favor.

When you leave work to go home, make sure your route goes past your gym. The sight of people exercising is often motivation enough, so make sure you have your workout gear with you. Not only that, but you can also give yourself a big pat on the back for having taken time out to exercise instead of going home and flopping down on the sofa.

If you don't feel like doing a full gym workout, have an alternative plan in place. Get off the train or the bus a stop earlier, or have your workout mat already set up in front of the TV and the workout DVD ready to go. If you have an alternative plan in place, you are twice as likely to have the motivation to work out, and you are twice as likely to actually do something instead of opting for the easy way out.

It is very easy for me to tell you to learn to see things in a more positive light, but that is exactly what you have to do. When something negative pops into your mind, change it into a positive thought. Think of another way of doing something. If you really can't get to the gym, exercise at home instead of giving it a miss altogether. Tell yourself that you can do those extra few minutes and that you can push yourself that little bit further.

Chapter 5: The Biggest Weight Loss Motivators

The single biggest motivator anyone should ever need for losing weight, eating a better diet, and working out more is their health. Obesity is a contributing factor to many different health conditions, and losing just 5% to 10% of your weight can result in massive benefits, both short and long term.

If sufficient weight can be lost to bring your body mass index back into a safe range and so that you are no longer classified as clinically obese, the benefits will be even bigger.

Some of the heath conditions caused by being overweight are:

- Type 2 diabetes
- Pre-diabetes
- Heart disease
- Arthritis, osteoarthritis, and other joint pain-related conditions
- Infertility

Losing weight can help you to:

- Avoid diabetes and control your blood glucose levels better
- Keep your heart healthy
- Sleep better
- Move better and eliminate pain in the joints
- Have better energy levels and feel more vitalized
- Have much better fertility

Let's look at each of these in turn:

Diabetes/Pre-Diabetes

Pre-diabetes is caused by high blood glucose levels, and this occurs when the glucose levels are much higher than normal, but not high enough that you can be officially classed as having diabetes. Type 2 diabetes is when the pancreas no longer produce sufficient amounts of insulin to meet the needs of your body, or the insulin that is produced is not doing its job properly. If you have pre-diabetes, you have a much higher chance of getting full-blown type 2 diabetes later on.

One of the leading risk factors for diabetes is obesity. Having to carry the excess weight makes it very hard work for your cells to respond in the proper way to the insulin that your body produces. This is because the fat that you carry is acting as a layer of insulation, and this makes it hard work for sugar to get into the cells. This results in more sugar or glucose circulating through your blood than there should be.

If you are diagnosed with pre-diabetes, you can work on preventing it from turning into type 2 diabetes by losing weight and keeping it off. Recent studies showed that if obese people were to lose 7% of their weight and do moderate activity, such as walking for a total of 150 minutes per week, they can either delay or prevent the onset of diabetes by around 58%.

Improving Blood Sugar Control

Excessive levels of sugar in the blood that is not controlled properly mainly cause complications in diabetes. The risk of suffering from chronic heart disease, heart attack, stroke, blindness, kidney failure, and even amputation of the legs is much higher for a person with type 2 diabetes, and this is as a direct result of the excessive sugar levels attacking the blood vessels and damaging them.

By controlling the levels of glucose in the blood, diabetic patients can prevent, or at least delay, some of these complications from occurring, but just lowering the level isn't enough. It has to be maintained and controlled very tightly, and one of the best ways to do this is to lose weight and get involved in a healthy eating and regular exercise program.

Keeping Your Heart Healthy

High blood pressure and high cholesterol are the two biggest risk factors for heart disease. Recent studies have found that when excess fat accumulates in the body, it will release chemicals that occur naturally into the bloodstream. These chemicals cause a rise in blood pressure, and the excess weight is what causes the liver to produce too much LDL cholesterol.

LDL cholesterol, or low-density lipoprotein, is known as bad cholesterol. It is sticky, and it settles in the blood vessel walls, which leads to the arteries narrowing down, causing a condition known as atherosclerosis. It is also a leading risk factor for stroke and heart attack. When a person loses weight, blood pressure tends to go lower, and the levels of LDL produced by the liver are reduced. The results from a study at the Royal Adelaide Hospital showed that a 10% reduction in LDL levels, a 12% reduction in total cholesterol levels, an 8% reduction in systolic blood pressure, and a 5% reduction in diastolic blood pressure could be achieved with weight loss.

Better Sleep

Overweight people are more likely to snore than those who are not overweight. Snoring is caused by the airways narrowing down, which obstructs the movement of air. Overweight people have a lot more soft neck tissue, which can increase the chances of snoring. However, snoring may also be one of the symptoms of a condition that can be life-threatening. I am talking about sleep apnea, a condition in which the person's airway is obstructed completely, causing inability to breathe. To start breathing again, the person has to wake up.

A person who has sleep apnea can wake any number of times throughout the night but will rarely remember doing so. The sleep and the oxygen deprivation can cause devastating health effects, including a severely compromised immune system, high blood pressure, heart disease, memory problems, and sexual dysfunction.

Losing weight can cut down on the amount of soft tissue in the neck and reduce snoring, and maintaining a good weight can encourage you to sleep better and reduce the risk of sleep apnea.

Studies have been conducted to see the effect of weight loss on how severe sleep apnea is, and it was found that losing 10% of your weight can decrease the level of sleep apnea events by 26% every hour. A further study was conducted obese people with type 2 diabetes and sleep apnea. It was found that those who reduced their weight were more than three times more likely to almost completely eliminate their sleep apnea episodes compared to those who did not lose any weight. Those who lost more than 10 kg in weight showed the greatest reduction of episodes per hour.

More Mobility and Less Pain in the Joints

Osteoarthritis is one of the most common joint disorders. The condition causes the bone and the cartilage that protects the joints to wear down; as a result, the joints can become tender and swollen. This can make movement painful, and being overweight will exacerbate this by putting more stress on the joints, especially the hips and knees. When you walk, an estimated force of between three and six times your weight is placed on the knee, so carrying an extra 10 kg in weight can equate to between 30 and 60 extra kilograms.

Losing just 5% of your body weight can cut down the stress on the hips, knees, and lower back and significantly cut down on pain. Remember that losing just 5 kg will equate to a reduction of between 15 and 30 kg of stress on these joints. In a loss of 10% of body weight, it has been shown that the symptoms of knee osteoarthritis can improve by 28%.

Improvements in Energy Levels and Vitality

When a person loses weight, we know that the physical levels are easily seen, but what many people do not think about is the psychological benefits. Studies have shown that when weight is lost, a person will benefit from a better quality of life, higher levels of energy, higher self-esteem, and lower rates of depression. This, in itself, is one of the greatest motivators.

Improvements in Fertility

It has been shown though numerous studies that obesity can have a serious effect on fertility and reproduction. Although the exact nature of the relationship between the two has not been shown, it is thought the excess of body fat can cause ripples in metabolizing the sex hormones that are responsible for the menstrual cycle.

It has also been reported that obesity during pregnancy can increase the chances of miscarriage and medical complications. Specifically, pregnancy-induced hypertension, gestational diabetes, thromboembolism, preeclampsia, and sleep apnea are the conditions most likely to occur.

In addition, deliveries for women who are obese may be further complicated by increased rates of caesarian section, labor induction, and a difficult labor because of the size of the baby. The babies born to overweight or obese women have a much higher rate of being admitted to neonatal intensive care and having congenital defects. Injuries during birth and fetal death are also more likely in obese cases, and babies are likely to have a much heavier birth weight, which puts both the baby and the mother at risk of trauma. The baby may also go on to suffer childhood obesity and possibly lifelong obesity.

Although there have been few studies conducted on the reproductive implications of losing weight in obese women who have problems with fertility, one study did show that even a small loss in weight for an obese woman who is infertile can raise the rate of ovulation, rate of pregnancy, and successful outcome of pregnancy.

Chapter 6: Motivational Quotes

Motivation really is the key to success in anything, and diet, fitness, and weight loss are not exceptions to that rule. This chapter is all about getting motivation in a different way – through inspirational quotes and through telling yourself that you will succeed.

9 Things to Say to Yourself to Stay on Track

Everyone makes mistakes, especially when it comes to sticking to a healthy lifestyle, but whether you missed a few workouts (or a lot) or you completely fell off your diet wagon, it doesn't take very much to get yourself back in the saddle again. All you need is motivation, and one way to get that is to surround yourself with inspirational quotes.

Whenever you read them, they should help you to channel that energy and to stay positive, banishing negative thoughts from your mind altogether. These are just some of the quotes you could write down on sticky notes and pop around your home or office for a little motivation when you feel you need some.

"Being defeated is only a temporary condition. Giving up is what makes it permanent."

You now that you were only going to pick up a cup of coffee to take to work this morning, but that muffin really did call out to you. When you fall prey to a craving, it could just be the temptation you need to ditch your diet for the rest of the day. Don't. Having one muffin is one thing, but throwing your healthy eating plan away and eating whatever takes your fancy for the rest of the day is not the answer. Savor that muffin, and then get straight back on track.

"Strive for progress, not perfection."

How many times did you hit the snooze button this morning? That last time meant missing out on your morning workout, but while you could probably give yourself a good kick, bear in mind that your entire weight loss and fitness goal does NOT depend on that one workout. Tomorrow is another day and another chance to work towards your goal. If you really feel that bad about it, fit in a walk at lunchtime or after work. In a few months' time, when you look back on your journey, you won't even remember the time you couldn't to the gym.

"Fall down 7 times, get up 8. Don't give up!"

For most of you, this definitely will not be your first time on the diet roundabout. Some people simply can't succeed on their first attempt, and it might take several. If you really do struggle to stick to a clean-food diet or just can't find the time to get to the gym, don't worry about it. The next time you try could just be the time when it all falls into place.

"Yes, you can! The road may be bumpy, but stay committed to the process."

You've been dead good; you've been to the gym and followed your routine on time every day for weeks, and then you bust your back. So, you can't get to the gym or do your normal routine for a few days, but hey, that doesn't mean sitting back and doing nothing. Go for a gentle walk, and then cook up a good healthy meal. Healthy lifestyles are made from lots of things, not just one, so don't give up when you come up against a stumbling block.

"Optimist: Someone who figured out that taking a step backward after taking a step forward isn't a disaster; it's more like a cha-cha."

Every day, the numbers on your scale go up, and then they go down, but you know, that's fine. This is all about living a healthier life, being happier and fitter, and not just about getting into that pair of skinny jeans you wore 5 years ago. Setbacks are everywhere in life, and you just have to deal with them, whether its missing out on a workout or giving in to temptation at the vending machine because you didn't have time for lunch. While you should always have your short-term goals in mind, you should always have your focus firmly on the long-term goals.

"It's how you handle the mistakes that creates your success."

So, all day long, you've stuck with the plan and eaten all that lovely healthy food. Then, you go home and fell into a block of cheese while you were making dinner. Don't beat yourself up over it. Instead, see it as the motivation you need to make improvements. You know when you will be at your most vulnerable to giving in to temptation, so make sure you are prepared for it. Have a healthy snack on hand to eat on the way home so that you don't walk through the door starving.

"Stay committed to your decisions, but stay flexible in your approach."

You are the one who made the commitment to leading a healthier life, but that doesn't mean that you are in control all the way. You can eat clean foods when it's you doing the cooking, but what about when you go out for a meal or to relatives who only eat packaged and processed foods? Instead of getting annoyed that you can't stick to your healthy diet, go with the flow and make the commitment to get back on track the next day.

"If you stumble, make it part of the dance."

So, you've given in and opted to try a new diet craze, but after a couple of days, you've already stumbled. This diet isn't for you because there is no way on earth you are giving up the cream in your coffee. Instead of throwing in the towel straight away, look at the diet as a whole. Is there any way that you can make that concession if the rest of the diet is going to work for you? Work out what you want and what your mind needs, and then stick to it.

More Motivational Quotes to Help You Through the Day

One of the most famous motivational quotes is: "Motivation is what gets you started, but habit is what gets you going." This is an accurate representation of how motivation fits into diet and fitness. Without it, you will not get the results you want, even if you follow a diet to a tee and stick to your fitness routine. The following are ten of the very best motivational quotes in the world.

"You can do it, even if it takes some time!"

"A huge part of losing weight is believing you can do it and realizing that it isn't going to happen overnight."

Weight loss and self-confidence are interlinked. When your confidence is high, you find it easier to lose weight because you believe in yourself. When you lose that weight, your self-confidence grows will grow because you will feel better. Believing is the force that drives you, but patience must be your guide. You don't lose weight overnight; it takes time. After all, you didn't gain it all overnight, did you?

"No More Excuses."

"No more excuses.

No more negative body thoughts.

No more, 'I'll do it tomorrow.'

No more sitting and wishing for a thinner me.

No more eating when I am not hungry.

No more waiting for this to get easier.

No more muffin tops.

No more wobbly thighs.

No more soft, round stomach.

No more 'buts...'

No more 'I can't...'

No more 'it's too hard...'

No more 'I'm too tired...'

NO MORE EXCUSES."

You know that there is no end to excuses that you could come up with as to why you can't start your diet just yet or why you can't make it to the gym. Excuses are for losers, and it's the winners who make and take the opportunities. When you find yourself thinking up an excuse, turn it around, and make it into something that you know you will be proud of tomorrow.

"What you do is who you want to be."

"The difference between who you are and who you want to be is what you do, and what you have to do to get where you want to be may not be pretty or may not come easy."

We fall into two categories – people who want more out of life and those who are happy to settle for a little less. When it comes to losing weight and getting fit, aim high, or you will get far less. Make your goals higher to gain greater benefits.

"No pain, no gain."

"No, your legs aren't that tired. Yes, you can breathe. Keep going."

The famous Muhammed Ali was once quoted as saying, "No, I don't count my sit-ups; I only start counting when it stars hurting because they're the only ones that count." Always aim to do more and push your limits. Get through the pain barrier, and the benefits will flow.

"Challenge is a step forward."

"If it doesn't challenge you, it doesn't change you."

If you ever find yourself in a situation that is a little unusual, it is because you are challenging yourself and your abilities. To go from spending your life slouched on a couch to being a top fitness fanatic is the biggest challenge you will ever face, so step up and take it on.

"Love yourself, and respect your body."

"I don't work out because I hate my body; I work out because I love it."

If you want to change the way your body looks, you must first accept it as it is now. Love your body, love how unique it is, and use your workouts to improve on it.

"Make the first step today."

"Every journey begins with a single step, but you'll never finish it if you don't start."

Pythagoras once said, "The beginning is half of the whole." When you take that first step, what follows will become easier. You have to take that first step though because you cannot finish something that you haven't started.

"Work for it."

"Don't wish for it; work for it."

While that first step is important, in order for you to be able to take it, you have to work hard for it – it isn't going to happen with a wave of a magic wand. In health and fitness, you have to work for your results and work hard; otherwise, your wish will stay exactly where it is now and will never become a reality.

"Are you a weight loss winner, or weight loss loser?"

"Winners find a way; losers find an excuse."

Which category do you want to be in? Are you with the winners or the losers? Think about it carefully, because it is as simple as that. You decide what you want to be and set the targets, or you claim defeat and walk away.

"Where do you want to go tomorrow?"

"You can feel sore tomorrow, or you can feel sorry tomorrow. You choose." – Unknown

Whatever you achieve today will be what sets up your feelings for the next day. Make your choice. Do you prefer to feel disappointed or satisfied? You need to make the decision today, because tomorrow, you may not be in the right frame of mind.

"Do What's Best for You."

"If you don't do what's best for your body, you're the one who comes up on the short end." – Julius Irving

What this comes down to is this: If you don't look after yourself, you will end up coming up short. Everything will suffer – your health, your body, and your mind, and ultimately, that means you will. You don't have to.

"Can't isn't the answer."

"Instead of giving myself reasons why I can't, I give myself reasons why I can." – Unknown

Put simply, "can't" is not a word that should be in your vocabulary, so eliminate it today.

"Don't give up."

"Never, never, never, never give up." – Winston Churchill

One of the most motivational speakers, Churchill came up with one of the simplest sentiments ever. Simply, don't ever give up, and don't ever stop trying.

"Always visualize."

"You must begin to think of yourself as becoming the person you want to be." – David Viscott

This is one of the truest motivational quotes ever. You should always see yourself as how you want to be, who you want to be, and how healthy you want to be.

"Try, and try again."

"The difference between 'try' and 'triumph' is just a little umph!"
– Marvin Phillips

This quote highlights how important it is to work hard and be determined because the end is worth the work.

"To your health!"

"The groundwork of all happiness is health." – Leigh Hunt

Healthy people are happy people. In working towards your weight loss goal, make health improvements your very first milestone because this will be what sees you through to end.

"Act now!"

"The time for action is now. It's never too late to do something."
– Carl Sandburg

How easy it is to put something off until tomorrow, but sometimes, tomorrow never comes. If you are struggling to get started, use this quote as a mantra you could keep repeating to yourself. Sometimes, we only get now to make a choice, so do it while the opportunity is there.

"Don't quit!"

"The man who can drive himself further once the effort gets painful is the man who will win." – Roger Bannister

At the end of the day, the only person you are competing against is you, but you should still keep this quote in mind. Losing weight is tough, and some days are harder than others, but when you give it all you've got – when you use all that will power and all that self-control – the rewards are great.

"Don't feel inferior."

"No one can make you feel inferior without your permission." – Eleanor Roosevelt

While Eleanor Roosevelt had a lot of wise things to say, this is perhaps one of the wisest. We all know that obesity carries its own stigma, but it really doesn't have to. You do not have to let anyone make you feel bad about anything

"Mind over matter."

"The good Lord gave you a body that can stand most anything. It's your mind you have to convince." – Vince Lombardi

This is perhaps one of the truest quotes ever because losing weight really is a case of mind over matter. If you feel thinner in your mind, you can think your way to being thin. Getting it straight in your mind is the beginning of your journey – from there, it gets easier.

I hope that at least some of these quotes will give you the motivation you need to continue on your journey. It is hard, but it is a rewarding journey. Regardless of the blips you may encounter along the way, keep these quotes in mind to give you the motivation to continue.

Chapter 7: Tips to Help You Stick to the Diet

It is difficult for anybody to change their lifestyle, and it is especially hard to stop eating the food you love to eat or even control what you eat. This chapter will look at some tips you can use to help you stick to your diet.

Avoid Skipping Breakfast

You do not lose weight if you skip breakfast. If you skip breakfast, you may miss some essential nutrients in the morning, forcing you to snack throughout the day because you are hungry. Having said that, if you choose to follow the intermittent fasting eating pattern, you can skip breakfast. Bear in mind that you need to stick to the eating pattern if you want to lose weight easily.

Eat Regularly

It is important to eat meals at regular intervals to burn calories faster. When you eat regular meals, you can reduce the temptation you feel. You can curb your cravings and manage your hunger pangs.

Eat More Fiber

It is important to increase your fiber intake if you want to improve your metabolism and reduce your hunger pangs. Fruits and vegetables are the best foods to include in your diet because they are low in fat and calories. They are also rich in fiber. These three ingredients are important if you want to lose weight. Fruits and vegetables both contain a lot of minerals and vitamins.

Foods with fiber keep hunger at bay. This is a good idea, especially if you want to lose weight. Fiber is found in most foods that come from plants, such as oats, brown rice, beans, lentils, peas, fruit, and vegetables.

Be Active

You need to stay active if you want to lose weight. It is especially important to do this if you want to manage weight loss. Exercise not only helps you lose weight but also has numerous benefits. It can help you burn any excess calories you eat throughout the day as well. If it is difficult for you to exercise regularly, choose an activity you love.

Hydrate

People are often thirsty when they feel pangs of hunger. You often consume too many calories when you could have stopped the hunger pangs by drinking a little water. So, ensure you drink enough water throughout the day to ensure you are not thirsty.

Read Labels

It is important to read food labels to ensure you choose the right options for you. Suppose you want to determine if you can consume a certain type of food; learn how to use the calorie information on the food label. Use the information to determine the effect of some foods on your weight loss.

Use Smaller Plates

If you want to reduce the quantity of food you eat, stick to using smaller plates. When you use smaller bowls and plates, your body will adapt and get used to eating smaller portions. You can sustain yourself throughout the day without feeling hungry. Your stomach takes 20 minutes to tell your brain that it is full. So, chew slowly, and do not eat any more food if you feel full.

Stop Avoiding Foods

If you ban foods from your diet, you will crave those foods. Do not remove foods you like from your diet. Banning only increases your craving because this is how your mind works. You can enjoy treats occasionally, but be sure to stick to your caloric intake.

Avoid Stocking Junk Food

You can avoid temptation if you do not stock junk food. You cannot eat too many biscuits, chocolate, and crisps. It is best to avoid soda and other carbonated drinks. Choose healthy snacks instead, such as unsalted rice cakes, fruit, oat cookies, popcorn, or juice. You can drink fruit or vegetable juice, but do not add too much salt and pepper.

Reduce Alcohol Intake

You may want to drink a glass of wine when you eat dinner. Did you know that one glass of wine and a piece of chocolate have the same number of calories? If you keep drinking a glass of wine during each meal, you are bound to gain weight.

Have a Meal Plan

It is best to plan your meals, including your snacks, for the entire week. Ensure you stick to your caloric intake and requirements. It is best to create a weekly shopping list and buy everything you need over the weekend.

Chapter 8: The Best Way to Start a Diet

It is a good idea to start a diet to lose weight because this improves your health. It is a worthy objective, but it is overwhelming to change everything about your life. You will face challenges when you begin anything new, and it is harder if you need to do this multiple times a day. This chapter has some secrets and tips to help you lose weight and keep that weight off. After all, what is the point of losing weight if you are only going to gain it all back again?

Choose a Healthy Plan

It is important to identify the right plan, and stick to it. This plan should include foods you love, along with other foods, such as vegetables, fruit, low-fat dairy, whole grains, seafood, lean meat, nuts, and beans. These foods have fewer calories when compared to other foods that can satisfy your cravings. These foods can help you stick to your diet and are rich in fiber. They are also low in fat and have enough protein.

You will slowly stop craving your favorite food, especially those high in calories and fats. A diet will help you control your intake of heavily processed foods and replace those foods with nutritious and healthy options. Bear in mind that you can change the foods you eat and the plan you follow if you need to. You can switch some foods for others if you want. You can change your plan at the end of a week or month, depending on how you feel.

Do not worry if you have intolerances, allergies, or are a vegetarian. You can include all the food groups recommended for you in your diet, but ensure that whatever you add provides the required nutrition. It is recommended that you take a multivitamin or mineral supplement in case you have any nutritional gaps.

Take Baby Steps

It is hard to change, and it is best to make small and gradual changes. Experts recommend that you change only one thing every week, so your body and mind get used to the idea of things changing. The objective is for you to develop and establish new habits that you can sustain for a lifetime.

The easiest way to do this is to stock your pantry and refrigerator with foods you should consume on your diet. You also need to plan your meals and eat something healthy. If you are unsure of what foods you can cook, buy a cooking magazine or cookbook specializing in a specific cuisine. If you still are not satisfied, join an online forum where people are discussing similar issues. Something on those websites is bound to help you.

Set Realistic Goals

It is hard for people to lose weight because they set unreasonable targets. They dream about fitting into old clothes or into clothing sizes that are not realistic. If you lose even 5% of your body weight or more, it changes the way you feel. You will find yourself motivated to do better and improve your health and wellbeing. Losing even a little weight helps to lower your blood sugar, cholesterol levels, and blood pressure.

It is best to set goals that are realistic and attainable. Experts recommend that you lose only one or two pounds each week. If you lose more, it is a sign of unhealthy weight loss. Bear in mind that slow and steady is the only way to go. It will take time for you to learn new eating habits, especially if you want to follow these for the rest of your life.

Use Rewards

As you maintain realistic and attainable goals, it is easy to meet them in the required time. It is best to reward yourself every time you reach a goal. If you exercise five times a week or lose five pounds, you need to pat yourself on the back. Find simple and effective ways to reward yourself.

You also should never be too hard on yourself if you cannot stick to your diet plan. It is important to remember that everybody has trouble with sticking to a new eating plan. If you do fall off the wagon, find a way to get back on track. Use this situation to identify what foods cause you to stop following your diet, and decide how you will take care of yourself in such situations without giving up. Experts recommend that you break the rules

20% of the time and adhere to them 80% of the time so you feel healthy.

Find a Buddy

It would help if you had someone to support you when you begin your weight loss plan. You can ask a friend or family member to support you. They may not want to partake in the diet plan, but you can ask them to work out with you or take a walk. If you do not want to ask your friends or family for help, join an online forum, and connect with people on the same journey. These people will be your source of support, encouragement, and inspiration. You can speak with them as often as you can, and it is better to have this support, especially when things get tough for you.

Track Your Intake

You need to know how much you eat in every meal. You need to document this to keep your intake in check. Write it down so you can control yourself. Use a diary or an application or tool to track your intake. Most applications give you a chance to measure your intake and track your consumption of nutrients.

Exercise!

I cannot emphasize this any more. Bear in mind that cutting your caloric intake and eating healthy is only a part of your success. If you really want to lose weight, you need to be active.

Through exercise, you not only lose weight by burning calories but also increase your coordination, strength, and balance. This reduces stress and improves your health and wellbeing.

It is best to get some exercise every morning, but ensure you do not overwork yourself. Do not squeeze in a workout in between your hectic schedule because this does not work for most people. Before you begin any new activity, speak with your doctor. You also need to discuss your eating plan to ensure you provide your body with enough nutrition to sustain you throughout the day.

Be proud of yourself. It is hard to change your lifestyle and eating patterns, and you should pat yourself on the back for making this decision. Bear in mind that the road ahead will have a lot of potholes and bumps, but if you have a good plan, the right attitude, and a support system, you are going to succeed.

Chapter 9: How to Stay Motivated

Have you started a diet recently but could not stick to it for longer than a week or maybe a month? Well, you are not the first person to go through this. The idea of sticking to a new diet plan or lifestyle does seem impossible, but this only happens if you do not have the motivation.

If you look back, you can determine exactly when you stopped following the diet. Now, if you think about the situation, you know you were no longer motivated to follow the diet, so you gave up. You can find different ways to motivate yourself, and this chapter includes some of the best ways to do so.

Define Why You Want to Follow the Diet

It is important to define why you want to lose weight. Grab a notebook, and make a note of these points. Keep this sheet close to you so you stay committed. This list will also motivate you and help you reach your goal. Read through this list regularly, and use it as a reminder, especially when you feel like straying from your plan.

You may have many reasons, such as keeping up with your kids or grandchildren, preventing the onset of diabetes, improving your self-confidence, looking great at an event, or fitting into your best clothing. Most people begin their weight loss plan when their doctor suggests that they lose weight. Research shows that people often lose weight faster if they are motivated for reasons that do not relate to a doctor.

Therefore, define your objectives or goals, and make note of them. Ensure you drive yourself to meet your goals because of how you feel from within.

Set Realistic Expectations

Most diet products and diets claim you can lose weight easily. Some may even help you lose weight in a week or two, but this is not healthy weight loss. Experts and nutritionists recommend you lose anywhere between 1 and 2 pounds a week. If you lose more than that, it is an indication of unhealthy weight loss. It is best to set attainable goals to avoid frustration. If you tell yourself you need to fit into a specific dress in less than two weeks, you are going to be annoyed.

When you set achievable goals and accomplish them, you feel a sense of accomplishment. Meeting self-determined and set goals often push you to work harder, and you are bound to lose more weight and stick to the diet plan for the long term.

A study conducted by Grave R D et al. in 2005 was based on weight loss data collected from different centers. According to the research team's analysis, women who did not set realistic goals and objectives often dropped out of their weight loss programs. The good news is that even a small loss in weight can go a long way. You will feel better after losing even a little weight. For instance, if you are 180 pounds and lose 18 pounds in 9 weeks, you will feel a lot better than you did a few weeks ago.

When you lose even 5% of your body weight, you can:

- Reduce the risk of developing certain types of cancers
- Improve and control blood sugar
- Lower your risk of heart diseases
- Alleviate joint pain
- Reduce cholesterol levels

So, learn to set realistic expectations when it comes to losing weight, so you can boost your sense of achievement and avoid burning out.

Focus on Your Process

Unfortunately, people do not realize that they should not only set outcome goals. It is also important for them to set process goals. An outcome goal is what you should achieve at the end of the program, which is usually the target weight. This method can affect your motivation because you do not know when you will reach that weight. You may have hit a plateau, and it will be hard for you to move past it. Outcome goals can leave you feeling overwhelmed because you can only achieve them after a period.

To avoid feeling this way, set process goals. Identify the actions you will take to reach the goal. For instance, you can say that you will work out at least four times a week while trying to lose weight. This is a process goal, and you can reward yourself once you meet it. You will also feel better about the process when you do this.

A study conducted by Pearson E S in 2012 had 126 overweight women as subjects. These women were all a part of different weight loss programs. Pearson noted that women who were a part of process-focused programs lost weight at the right pace and did not lose motivation. Unlike the women who were focused only on the outcome goals, they did not move away from their diets.

Therefore, you need to set SMART goals for yourself:

- Specific
- Measurable
- Attainable
- Realistic
- Time-based

Consider the following examples of SMART goals or process goals you should have:

- I will walk for at least 30 minutes every day for a week.
- I will limit snacking to only one day a week.
- I will not drink soda this week.

Choose a Plan that Suits Your Lifestyle

You must find a plan that is easy for you to stick to. Do not choose plans that you cannot follow easily in the future. There are a lot of diets out there, and most of these are based on calorie counting. When you create a calorie deficit in your body, it will help you lose weight. Dieting, however, especially if you constantly switch from one diet to the other, can lead to weight gain in the future. Therefore, you should focus on the type of diet you choose to follow. Never follow a diet that expects you to eliminate certain foods completely.

A study conducted by Teixiera P J et al. in 2012 concluded that people could not follow a diet or a dietary pattern if they needed to eliminate foods. When you eliminate foods from your diet, your body begins to crave them, and this will make it harder for you to stick to your diet. Work on developing a plan that works for you. Keep the following tips in mind when you prepare the plan:

- Increase your intake of fruits and vegetables
- Decrease your caloric intake
- Reduce desserts and fried food
- Reduce portion sizes
- Reduce the frequency of snacks

Maintain a Journal

It is important to monitor yourself if you want to lose weight successfully. As mentioned earlier, self-monitoring is one way to motivate yourself to stick to your diet. A study conducted by Kong A et al. in 2012 had people who were in weight loss programs as subjects. Some subjects were asked to maintain a journal, while others did not. The research team found that people who tracked their food intake were able to lose weight faster. They also found it easier to maintain their weight loss.

Having said that, it is important to make notes correctly if you choose to maintain a food journal. You need to write everything down. This means you need to include details of all your snacks, meals, and even the slice of cake you ate at work. If you want to make the process effective, note down your emotions, too. This information will help you identify any triggers causing you to binge or overeat. Use this information to learn how to cope with such situations.

You can either use an application or website to maintain a food journal. These are known to be effective.

Apps to Use as Food Journals

Food does not affect your weight alone. It also affects your health, mood, and various lifestyle factors. The following are some applications that you can use to track your intake, and it may seem like a pain to do this, especially because you may snack. It is a good habit to maintain a food journal and identify everything you consume. You need to know what you are putting into your body. This is honestly a great way for you to learn more about yourself.

Some of the best food diary applications you can use are listed below. Each of these follows a different approach, so choose the one that works best for you.

- **See How You Eat**

This app is compatible with both Android and iOS. It is a visual food diary, which means you need to take pictures of everything you eat. This is the easiest way to maintain a food journal. This application is still a work in progress, but it is great if you are only starting off with maintaining a food journal.

The objective of the application is to avoid calorie counting. Most food diary applications use calorie counting, and this is a turn-off for most people. This application does not require you to do anything more than taking a picture of the food you are eating. If you are new to this, you may forget to do this, so the application reminds you. This way, you can remember to take pictures whenever needed.

The objective is for you to take a picture of everything you send into your body, which means you need to take a picture of the glass of water you are drinking, too. You can only upload 12 pictures a day, and there are some bugs, too. The application, however, works well if you want to develop the habit of tracking your intake.

- **YouEat**

This app can also be used on both Android and iOS. This is an amazing food journal and tracker application, which expects you to chart the path of every meal you eat. You can also use this application to determine why you ate a certain meal. Using this application, you can identify the triggers that made you eat a specific type of food. You can also determine why you did not stick to your diet plan.

Let us look at how the application works. You click a picture of the food you are eating and either put it on your off-path or on-path. I am sure you know the path being referred to; on-path refers to food on your diet plan. Meanwhile, if you eat something you should not have, add it to your off-path list. When you add this to the off-path, you also need to indicate why you ate that meal. Was it because you were upset, angry, hungry, stressed, or anxious? Did you eat the food because you were craving something? It is important to add notes, so you are aware of why you behave a certain way.

If you use the application regularly and accurately, this becomes a great way for you to determine why you choose certain foods and the reason for choosing those foods. It is important to add these reasons to identify what makes you eat certain foods and why you chose to break your diet. It is this information that can help you stick to your weight loss plan. You can also use a recipe management application to track the foods you eat or if you want to learn some new recipes.

- **RiseUp**

RiseUp is an app you can use on both Android and iOS. Using this application, you can determine how certain foods affect your mood. This application understands that the food you eat affects you mentally. This is especially true if you have any disorder. The application allows you to track all the food you ate and how you felt after eating the food. You can also track how you felt before you ate the food, giving you a pattern.

RiseUp also has a meal log, which you can use to add the food you ate when you ate it, whether you ate alone or with someone else, and how you ate it. You can also add information about how you felt during your meal. The application comes with some target behaviors that you can use to determine how you act after a meal, such as binge eating or weighing yourself. The objective of this application is to help you identify any patterns about yourself.

The application reminds you to check on yourself and your emotions frequently. It also expects you to check in with yourself and understand how you think and feel. When you combine this data, you get an idea of how your food intake affects the way you behave and act.

- **Cara**

Cara is an advanced app that comes with a full-body tracker. You can download this on both iOS and Android. If you have been using food journals for quite some time, this is the application for you. Use it if you want to connect with your water and food consumption. Use the information on the application to help you connect the food you eat with different symptoms in your life. The application also tracks various factors, and you can use this information to understand your thoughts and habits easily.

Like other applications, this also requires you to add notes every time you drink or eat something. The application does not come with any drop-down menus. You need to type everything out and take a photo if you feel like it. Unlike most food applications, this tracks your water intake, as well. If you do not drink enough water, it can affect your health in various ways, so the application also reminds you to drink enough water.

The application also allows you to add other factors, such as digestion, stool, mental status, supplements, and mediation. You can also track your period frequency, workout frequency, sleep patterns, skin condition, pain, and other information. After a point, the application will identify a pattern between your food consumption and health. So, the application can tell you how eating a bar of chocolate will make you feel.

- **MyPlate**

MyPlate is a very simple app used as a calorie counting application. LiveStrong developed it, which means you have an entire community to motivate you and push you to achieve your goals. This application is like other fitness applications where you count calories, but its interface is easier to use and better when compared to other applications.

You need to key in your goals – both outcome and process goals – into the application. It also allows you to add information about your sodium and calcium intake. The next step is to log every piece of food you eat. The database has over two million foods, and you can choose the food from this list. Alternatively, you can use the barcode to identify the food you are eating. MyPlate will calculate the nutritional break-up and calories by using the information you have keyed in.

The application is like other fitness applications, such as HealthifyMe, Lifesum, and MyFitnessPal. You can use any of these applications if you prefer them to MyPlate. If you have not tried any of these applications, choose MyPlate because it is easier to start with it.

- **Celebrate**

It is hard to lose weight, so it is important to celebrate when you achieve your goals. This is the easiest way to motivate yourself to stick to the diet plan. When you accomplish a goal, you need to reward yourself. If you do not have anybody to tell this to, you can post it on a weight loss forum, community page, or social media. These are great places for you to share how you are doing. People on these platforms are willing to lend support. You will also feel better about yourself, which will motivate you.

You should also celebrate any changes in behavior; this is not only if you reach the target weight. For instance, if you walked for thirty minutes five days this week, go out with your friends or celebrate at home. Rewarding yourself is a great way to increase motivation. It is important to choose the right rewards. Do not use food as a reward because that will only throw you off your diet. Do not choose expensive items as rewards, either, as you cannot buy all of them. It is also important to never choose something insignificant because then you would not want to buy it.

Some examples of rewards are:

- Taking a cooking class
- Getting a manicure

- Buying a new running top
- Going to a movie

Find Support

You may need to find support groups or people who will support you on your journey. This is another great way to stay motivated. Speak with your close friends and family members about your plan, and ask if they can help you on your journey. Most people find it easier to lose weight when they have a partner. This way, you can work out together and encourage each other. You can also monitor what the other person is doing.

It is best to have support from your family because you all eat together. Having said that, you need someone outside of your family to support you, too. Alternatively, you can join an online support group or an offline one, depending on what works best for you. These groups are beneficial because every member of the group is willing to listen to you.

Commit to the Plan

A study conducted by Hayes S C et al. in 1985 noted that people who committed to anything publicly were more likely to stick to their plan and follow it through. When you tell people around you about your plan to lose weight, they may extend their support on social media. If you share your goals with more people, you will be held accountable. You can also invest in an exercise package or gym membership. As you made an investment, you will be more likely to follow through and meet your goals.

Ooze Positivity

If you have positive expectations, you will feel confident about yourself. You know you can achieve your goals and meet your ideal or target weight. You can use a concept called change talk to motivate you to achieve your goals. Change talk is where you make a statement about committing to changing some behaviors. You can also write down why you want to make this change and how you will make it. This means you need to talk positively about your plans to lose weight. You can also talk about the various processes you will begin and how you will commit to your goals.

Having said that, if you fantasize about your goals without actually doing anything to achieve them, you are not going to achieve your goals. This is a process called mental indulging, and it does more harm than good. You should use a process called mental contrast to change the way you behave and think about your weight loss plan. Spend some time every day to imagine how you will feel if you reach your goals. You can also spend some time imagining the different hurdles that can come your way and find a way to overcome them.

A study conducted by Benyamini Y and Raz O in 2007 had 134 students as subjects. The researchers asked some students to use mental indulging and others to use mental contrast to understand their goals. Students who used mental contrast acted faster when compared to those who did not. They reduced their caloric intake, avoided high-calorie food, and exercised often.

Based on this study, we can conclude that people who use mental contrast can better motivate and push themselves to meet their goals when compared to those who use mental indulging. Using the latter technique, you can trick your brain into believing that you have achieved your goal, and this will cause you not to do anything.

Plan for Any Setbacks and Hurdles

You are going to have regular stressors, and you need to plan for them. Work toward developing the right coping skills to ensure you stick to your plan and motivate yourself no matter what happens in your life. There will be parties, holidays, and birthdays to attend. You are also going to have stressors in your family and at work. Therefore, you need to brainstorm and find a way to overcome these stressors without breaking off from your weight loss plan. This is the only way you can motivate yourself and stay on track.

Most people cave in under stress and reach for their comfort food. This means they abandon their weight loss plan. It is important to develop the right coping skills if you want to avoid this.

A study conducted by Elfhag K and Rössner S in 2005 concluded that people could handle stress if they have the right strategies. They can use these strategies to help them lose weight easily and maintain their weight. Some means to cope with stress include:

- Go outside and get some fresh air
- Exercise
- Practice square breathing

- Ask for help
- Call a friend
- Take a bath

It is also important to plan for social events and holidays. You cannot expect never to eat out. If you are keen on maintaining your diet, choose the place when you meet your friends. If you are at a party and cannot find food you can eat, go for smaller portions, and choose healthier foods.

Learn to Forgive Yourself

Bear in mind that you are human and bound to make mistakes. You cannot expect to do everything correctly. So, do not strive for perfection. As mentioned earlier, an all-or-nothing attitude will just make it harder for you to lose weight. If you restrict yourself too much, you will cave in every time some good food comes into view. For instance, if you see your colleagues grabbing a burger and fries outside work, you will cave in and eat that with them. You will later tell yourself that you can eat a pizza for dinner because you ate a burger for lunch. Instead of doing this, you need to tell yourself to eat a healthy dinner because you had a big lunch.

Do not beat yourself up if you make a mistake. If you have self-defeating thoughts, you cannot work toward your goal. Learn to forgive yourself, and remember that a small mistake will not make it hard for you to lose weight. Simply start from where you left off.

Appreciate and Love Your Body

A study conducted by Elfhag K and Rössner S in 2005 showed that people who had body image issues could not lose weight easily. It is important to change the way you perceive yourself if you want to lose weight easily or maintain your weight loss. People who have a better view of their body can pick a diet or weight loss plan and stick to it. They also try new activities that will help them meet their goals. One of the following can help you change the way you perceive your body:

- Appreciate and understand that your body is doing a lot for you.
- Exercise.
- Get a manicure, pedicure, or massage.
- Do something you love.
- Find a group of positive people, and stick with them.
- Avoid comparing yourself with people who are thinner than you. Do not compare yourself with models because you do not know what they did to look the way they do.
- If you find something that fits and you like it, wear it.
- Say things about yourself out loud when you look at yourself in the mirror.

Choose Activities You Enjoy

Exercise is an important aspect when it comes to weight loss. It will improve your wellbeing and help you lose weight. It is best to choose an exercise or activity you love doing, especially if you have had trouble sticking to it in the past. There are different ways and types of exercise, so explore different options, and identify what works best for you.

It is also important to determine where you would like to work out. Would you prefer working out inside the house or outside? Do you want to work out in your house or at the gym? It is also important to determine if you like exercising with a group of people or exercising alone. If you need motivation, pick a group class because the people around you can motivate you. If you do not like group classes, then you can work out at home, too.

Experts recommend you listen to music when you work out because that can motivate you. People exercise for longer when they listen to music.

Choose Your Role Model

It is best to have a role model if you want to motivate yourself to lose weight. Having said that, you should choose the right role model so you can meet your expectations. If you use pictures of supermodels to motivate you, you are not doing anything good for yourself. Choose a role model with whom you can relate. Choosing a positive and relatable role model will motivate you. You may have a friend who recently lost a lot of weight, and that friend can be your role model. If you have no idea who your role model should be, read some inspirational stories and blogs to learn about people who lost weight successfully.

Get a Dog

Yes! You read that right. Get yourself a dog because he can be your companion. A study conducted by Kushner R F in 2008 concluded that a dog could help you lose weight easily. If you own a dog, your physical activity increases because you have to take him for a walk frequently.

Another study conducted by Brown S G and Rhodes R E in 2006 concluded that people who owned dogs walked at least 300 minutes every week, and people who did not have dogs only walked 168 minutes.

Dogs also support you when you work out. They love it when there is any physical activity involved and may mimic you when you work out. An added bonus is that having a pet lowers blood pressure, reduces feelings of depression and loneliness, and lowers cholesterol. This means that having a dog not only makes life happier but also improves your physical and mental wellbeing.

Consult a Professional

Never hesitate to speak with a professional to help you with your plan and efforts. It is only when you are confident about your plan that you will lose weight. You can find a nutrition specialist or dietician to determine which foods you can eat. Alternatively, you can meet a physiologist if you want to learn how to exercise properly.

People often do better when they are accountable to a professional. If it is hard to motivate yourself, meet a dietician or psychologist who can motivate you. This is a great way for you to achieve your goals.

Chapter 10: Morning Habits to Help You Lose Weight

Regardless of your outcome goals, it is hard for people to lose weight, especially if they hit a plateau. That said, you do not have to change your diet and lifestyle entirely if you want to lose weight. It is easy to lose weight if you make a few changes to your routine. This chapter will look at ten habits you should incorporate into your morning routine if you want to lose weight.

Eat Protein-Rich Foods for Breakfast

There is a reason why people say you should eat breakfast. It is the most important meal because your body would have been fasting all night. The food you consume for breakfast will determine the food you eat throughout the day. Your breakfast determines if you are full until lunch or need to hit the snack bar at work for something at 11 a.m.

If you eat a high-protein meal, it can reduce cravings until lunch and help you lose weight. A study conducted by Hoertel H A et al. in 2014 concluded that adolescents, especially girls, who ate a protein-rich breakfast lose weight easily because the meal curbed their cravings. Another small study conducted by Leidy J H et al. in 2014 concluded that a high-protein breakfast ensured you do not gain too much fat as you are less hungry throughout the day.

Protein can reduce the levels of the hunger hormone ghrelin in your body, and this can decrease your appetite. Another small study conducted by Blom A M W et al. in 2006 had 15 men as subjects. Some were asked to consume a protein-rich breakfast while others ate a normal meal. It was found that a high-protein breakfast was more effective in lowering the levels of ghrelin in the body. If you want to start your day on a good note, eat eggs, cottage cheese, chia seeds, nuts, and Greek yogurt.

Hydrate

This is very important to bear in mind. It is best to begin your day with one or two glasses of water. This is an easy way to make it easier to lose weight. Water can increase the rate at which your body burns calories for at least an hour. A study conducted by Boschmann M et al. in 2003 concluded that drinking at least 500 ml of water every day when you wake up increases your metabolic rate by 30%. They further noted that people who drank water immediately after they woke up reduced their caloric intake by 13%.

Another study conducted by Stookey D J et al. in 2008 used overweight women as subjects. The women were asked to increase their water intake by one liter every day, and they lose at least 4 pounds more than people who did not increase their water intake. They were not asked to make any changes to their diet or exercise more.

When you drink water, it reduces your food intake and appetite. Research shows that it is best to drink at least 1.5 liters of water every day if you want to lose weight. It is best to start with a glass of water every morning and hydrate yourself throughout the day if you want to lose weight without making too much of an effort.

Measure Yourself

Another good thing to do is to measure your weight every morning. This is an effective way to motivate yourself. You can also improve your control and avoid eating foods that you should not. Several studies and research show that people lose weight faster when they weigh themselves every morning. A study conducted by Steinberg M D et al. in 2015 used 47 adults as subjects. The researchers noted that people who weighed themselves regularly for over six months lost weight faster than those who did not weigh themselves enough.

Another study conducted by VanWormer J V et al. in 2012 reported that adults who weighed themselves every morning lost 10 pounds in two years while those who did not gained weight. The latter only weighed themselves once a month. When you weigh yourself regularly, you will develop healthy behaviors and habits to help you lose weight. Another study was conducted by Butryn M L et al. (2007) on a large group of adults. Some adults were asked to weigh themselves regularly, while others were asked to stop weighing themselves. At the end of the study, the researchers concluded that the latter group did not have self-discipline and increased their caloric intake.

It is best to weigh yourself when you wake up, and you need to do this immediately after you use the bathroom and before you drink or eat anything. It is also important to understand that your weight will fluctuate regularly, and this is because of various factors. Therefore, you need to focus on your outcome and look for the trends. Do not worry about the changes that happen regularly.

Get Some Sunlight

Experts recommend you open the curtains every morning for sunlight. This is a great way to kick-start your metabolism. All you need to do is sit under the sun for a few minutes. A study conducted by Reid K J et al. in 2014 concluded that even limited exposure to the sun during the day could help you lose weight. Experts also believe that ultraviolet radiation can control or suppress weight gain, but further research is needed to confirm the same.

When you expose yourself to enough sunlight every day, you can meet your daily requirement for vitamin D. Research shows that your consumption of vitamin D directly impacts your weight. It can prevent weight gain, thereby helping you maintain your weight.

Mason C et al. conducted a study in 2014 where 218 obese and overweight women were the subjects. These women were either given a placebo or a vitamin D supplement for a year. Based on their findings, the researchers concluded that women who met their daily vitamin D requirement lost 7 pounds more than women who did not meet the requirement.

Another study conducted by LeBlanc E S et al. in 2012 had 4,659 older women as subjects and tracked them for four years. They found that people with more vitamin D in their bodies did not gain too much weight.

Your skin type determines the time you need to spend under the sun. Having said that, it is a good idea to let some sunlight into your house or sit outside for a few minutes every day.

Be Mindful

Mindfulness is a technique used to stay in the present and focus on what is happening around you. It is about being aware of your feelings and thoughts. This technique can promote healthy eating habits and aid in weight loss. For instance, an analysis performed by Carrière K et al. in 2018 showed that mindfulness-based methods or techniques helped people stop eating too much food. They also noted that incorporating mindfulness into a weight loss program could increase the chances of losing weight by 68%.

It is easy to practice mindfulness. If you want to start, all you need to do is spend a few minutes every morning to connect with your senses and learn to focus on the present.

Exercise

Exercising in the morning is the best way for you to lose weight. Alizadeh A et al. conducted a study in 2015 with a group of 50 obese women as subjects. These women were asked to perform different aerobic exercises at different times of the day. There were no differences identified between the food cravings of women who exercised in the afternoon when compared to the food cravings of women who exercised in the morning. However, the research team noted that women who exercised in the morning were not as hungry as women who exercised at a later part of the day.

When you exercise in the morning, you can maintain your blood sugar levels, thus reducing any hunger pangs or cravings. A study conducted by Gomez A M et al. in 2015 concluded that people who have type 1 diabetes have less trouble with blood sugar control during the day if they work out in the morning. These studies focused only on certain populations and did not discuss causation. Further research is needed to determine when people should exercise.

Change Your Mode of Transport

It is easy to drive to work or anywhere else you may need to go. This is not great for your visceral or abdominal fat. Research shows that using public transportation, walking, and biking is probably the best way to lose weight and reduce the risk of gaining weight. A study conducted by Sugiyama T et al. in 2013 followed 822 subjects for a period of four years. The research team found that people who often traveled by car were more obese compared to those who did not.

Another study conducted by Flint E et al. in 2014 followed a group of 15,777 people and concluded that using public or active methods of transport, such as biking or walking, helped to lower body fat percentage and body mass index when compared to using cars. Work on changing your mode of transport at least twice or thrice a week.

Focus on Your Intake

I know you know this by now, but this is an important point to bear in mind. It is only when you track your intake that you can lose weight easily. When you focus on the foods you eat, you learn to hold yourself accountable. Research shows that tracking your food helps you lose weight easily. You know exactly what you are putting into your body and know what needs to be done to lose weight.

A study conducted by Anton D S et al. in 2012 concluded that people who used a system to track their food intake and monitor their exercise and diet lost weight faster than the people who did not track this information. Another study conducted by Peterson D N et al. in 2015 used 220 overweight and obese women as subjects. The research team concluded that consistent and frequent use of self-monitoring applications and tools helped these women lose weight easily.

You can use an application or even maintain a diary to list the foods you drink and eat.

Chapter 11: Small Lifestyle Changes to Lose Weight

It may feel at times that you can lose weight only when you starve or deprive your body of calories, but this is not the case. The author of "Small Steps to Slim," Ashvini Mashru, says, "Healthy, sustainable weight loss is best achieved through small changes to your existing lifestyle." She reminds everybody that weight loss is a process. It is not a sprint, and you cannot lose weight in five days.

It is easier to adopt fad diets as you can drop a size in less than a week, but you are not going to stick to these diets in the long run. The weight will definitely drop quickly, but you will gain all the lost weight and more in a very short time if you do not take care of yourself. This chapter has some tips you can use to ensure you healthily lose weight. These are small lifestyle changes you can make to ensure you maintain or improve your health despite losing weight.

Focus on the Portions

According to Mashru, most Americans do not stick to their portion sizes. They eat twice the amount they should. Restaurants serve large portions of food, which will train your brain into thinking this is the amount of food you need to eat. If you want to understand your portions better, you should check the nutritional labels and understand the information given on those labels.

Pause Between Bites

You must chew slowly, as this is a simple way to lower your caloric intake. If you take time to chew instead of swallowing your food quickly, your body will feel full faster. Experts believe it takes your body only 20 minutes to feel full and for this feeling to reach your brain. If you eat slowly, you can relish the meal and eat less than you used to.

Prepare Your Lunch

When you prepare your lunch, you can save a lot of money, ensuring you are aware of what you are consuming. If you work from home, you can walk up to the fridge, pick up your box of food, and heat it up in the oven. Do not skip your meal. You may lose weight faster if you deprive your body of calories, but this only means you will overdo it later during the day or week.

Focus While Eating

If there is a lot of work to do or your friend has sent you a reel on Instagram, you may want to eat quickly to get to your laptop or phone. When you are distracted while you eat, you tend to eat more than you should. Distractions can force you to eat more throughout the day.

Snack Smartly

If you are trying to lose weight, you need to snack smartly. Snacking is helpful as long as you check what you eat. You may consume more than what you should when you snack because you do not know the number of nutrients you consume. This is a simple issue to fix because you can pre-pack your snacks and portion them according to your caloric intake. Another problem with snacking is that you may eat something throughout the day without realizing what it is that you are doing. It is important to focus on your goal and manage your intake.

Sleep Well

I am sure you want to catch up on episodes of *Friends* or watch the movie *Without Remorse*. This does not mean you do not sleep enough. It is important to sleep well and get enough rest if you want to lose weight. The appetite hormones leptin and ghrelin are kept in check if you sleep enough. If you do not sleep enough, you will have an imbalance in your body, increasing your appetite. Aim to sleep for at least 7 hours every night.

Healthy Eating at All Times

Your weekend cannot be your cheat day. You cannot eat whatever you want because it is the weekend. If you do this regularly, you will not lose weight the way you hoped you would. Eating poorly on weekends and not exercising is like taking 12 days off in a month, and this is not going to help with weight loss. Do not let the days of the week change the way you eat or behave. Focus on your healthy lifestyle, and ensure you sustain yourself throughout the week.

Use Small Plates

How does the same quantity of food look to you on a small plate when compared to a large plate? Your eyes will convince you that the smaller plate has more food. This is because of the Delboeuf illusion, which shows that empty space around anything will make it seem a little smaller. You may not be eating too much, but if you cut back on the space you have on your plate, you can convince your brain that you have eaten enough food. If you do the opposite, your brain may push you into thinking you are hungry, and this will only make you eat more.

Avoid Family-Style Eating

When you eat with your family, your table is filled with dishes with delicious food. You may mindlessly fill your plate with more food in such situations because everybody is eating, and the food is right there. If it is possible, you should avoid cooking too much food. Limit the quantity of food on your table. This does not mean you cannot take seconds, but it does mean you need to check if you are hungry before you go in for the second helping.

Do Not Face the Buffet

If the food in the restaurant is in your line of sight, you are going to feel terrible about missing some food. You may want to get your money's worth when you go to a restaurant. Instead of eating what is on your plate while looking at what you can eat next, focus only on what is on your plate. The buffet is not going anywhere, so you can eat more food if you want to.

Eat Enough Vegetables

When you follow a diet, you need to add things to your diet instead of removing them. This is a healthy way to look at a diet. If you do not consume any food you want to eat, you will binge on it, and this will only throw you off your plan. Instead of removing food from your diet, add more vegetables to your plate gradually. This will increase your chances of losing weight. Vegetables are rich in nutrients and also keep your body energized and healthy. They satiate your hunger and keep cravings at bay. If you want to avoid hating vegetables, start off small. Add one cup of vegetables to your meal for a week, and slowly increase the quantity when you get used to them.

Chapter 12: How to Create a Customized Diet Plan to Help You Lose Weight

If you want to lose weight healthily, you need to create a diet plan that works best. You must ensure your body receives the required calories and nutrients to sustain itself throughout the day, especially if you work out. It is important to maintain this balance if you want to get rid of fat and lose weight.

Your diet plan is successful if you consume the required nutrients, especially protein, to ensure your body builds muscle and maintains your energy. To do this, you need to understand your body and develop a plan that suits your needs. Use the steps in this chapter to develop a weight loss plan structured to your goals, habits, and lifestyle.

Step One: Do Not Use Calorie-Counting Diets

Most diet plans begin with setting a daily calorie limit. If you follow these diets, you need to reduce your consumption of any food you eat so that you fall within this limit. You need to eat healthy foods, so your body thrives. Unfortunately, this theory is what keeps dieters from sticking to their meal plans. They fail even before they start the diet. You need to look at different approaches to count your caloric intake.

Do you know why it is wrong to count your caloric intake every day?

- Bear in mind that every food you eat has a different number of calories. Unless you eat the same food every day, you cannot track your consumption easily. You would need to put in a lot of work, and this will throw you off

- Dieters cannot follow their diet when they go out with their friends or are on vacation. There are also other reasons why people cannot stick to their diet, one of which is that they cannot stick to their daily caloric count.

- To avoid temptation, some people designate some days as cheat days when they could eat everything they want to without worrying about their caloric intake. This is why some people do not lose weight even when they follow a low-calorie diet, especially as they over-indulge on one day.

- If you count your caloric intake regularly, you will eat less. However, most dieters choose to stay below the required caloric number, and because they miss too many calories regularly, they experience some negative effects

The objective should not be to set the number of calories you consume per day but rather to identify a plan that covers your necessities. Ensure you consume the required nutrients if you want to lead a healthy lifestyle. This is a good approach to follow when you want to lose weight. It is not restrictive and gives you enough freedom to eat the food you love in moderation.

Bear in mind that the nutritional needs of your friends and family are different from yours. These needs are based on your activity levels, weight, height, age, and medical needs. If you set the right guidelines and goals for yourself, you can eat different foods that will help you reach your goals. These goals enable you to focus on your intake of carbs, protein, minerals, vitamins, and fats. It is important to balance these nutrients to ensure your body has all the nutrition it needs.

Step Two: Calculating Your Macros

It is important to understand that dieting does not mean you control your food intake alone. Your body needs to get the right nutrition to grow muscle, burn fat, and provide enough energy to sustain you throughout the day. Your body uses macronutrients, such as carbohydrates, protein, and fat, to complete these tasks. These macronutrients constitute a major chunk of your caloric intake.

- **Carbohydrates**

Both complex and simple carbohydrates are sugar chains broken down by your body to provide energy to your organs and muscles.

- **Fats**

If you consume too many calories, your body stores them in fat cells and uses them in case of an emergency. If there are no carbohydrates that your body can burn, it will use these fat cells to produce energy. This energy is used by your body to perform hormonal and neural functions.

- **Proteins**

Proteins are known as the powerhouse macros because they provide your body with the energy it needs to grow and repair tissues.

It is important to balance these nutrients if you want to build a body that is not exhausted all the time. These nutrients also ensure you do not feel deprived of energy. A rule of thumb is that you need to divide your caloric intake as follows: 25% carbohydrates, 35% healthy fat, and 40% protein. You can speak with your nutritionist or doctor if you need a better measurement.

Step Three: Find Foods That Suit You

When you are aware of the quantity you need to eat, take some time to identify which foods fall into this category. Identify the foods you can regularly consume when you change your eating patterns. This is an effective way to lose weight because you only include foods in the diet if you can eat them. If you do not enjoy the food, you will not stick to your plan. Having said that, you need to make an effort to identify new options for your plan. Most dieters choose a weight loss program because they follow diets that limit their food intake and calories. It is essential to add more nutritional options and foods to your diet to create a long-term plan.

Make a list of all ingredients and foods you can eat. If you love something, add that to the list, too. When you begin your diet, you can add new fruits, grains, or vegetables to your plan each week. Experts recommend you include some information about the macronutrients in the foods you consume as this will help you determine whether you will enjoy your meals.

Step Four: Find Every Recipe You Can

You are now aware of the quantity of food you can eat and what you should eat. So, begin collecting a few recipes that include your preferred ingredients. Read the recipes, and understand them fully. The micronutrient content is dependent on the way you cook your food.

If you do not want weight loss to become boring, you should collect enough recipes. If you lose interest in your current menu, switch it up with other recipes. There are many reasons why people do not meet their target weight, and one of the most important ones is getting bored with the current meal plan. If you have variety, you will enjoy your meals and look forward to eating something new. You have numerous resources online, so use them to your benefit.

If you perform enough research, you can tweak and tailor any recipe you love to suit your needs. If you love pastries and cakes, find a recipe that falls within your calorie range. You do not have to quit eating foods you love because you are on a diet. You should only swap some ingredients or reduce the quantity of every ingredient you use. If you are worried about giving up fries, you can find a recipe that uses an oven to create a crispy outer covering.

If you lead a stressful life, compile a list of restaurants that serve food that meets your nutrient requirements. You can also meet the staff and ask for additional information if you want. You can use the information you have to identify a list of restaurants you can visit within your budget.

Step Five: Set a Schedule

It is important to determine when you eat, as this is as important as choosing what to eat. Your body constantly works and has a cycle, which affects your metabolism. There is a cycle that specifically works on your metabolism, and medical conditions can change the way that cycle works. This means you might not lose as much weight as you once hoped.

A diet plan includes three meals for most people, but this does not always work, especially for those who want to cut back on their caloric intake. It is best to have meals at regular intervals. Do not give your body too much of a gap between each meal during the day. You can give yourself a three-hour window between each meal. This will keep your hunger at bay and prevent you from eating unhealthy food. The following are some ways to help you develop a plan:

- Eat a heavy dinner if you want to avoid snacking at night
- Eat a high-protein breakfast an hour after you wake up
- Stick to the meal plan

If you have any glucose conditions or diabetes, speak with a dietician or nutritionist to know what you should eat. Ensure you develop a plan that works best for your body.

Step Six: Track, Adjust, and Analyze

As mentioned earlier, maintaining a food journal can go a long way. You can keep track of your meal plan and maintain a record of the food you eat. This gives you a chance to understand your eating habits and determine whether your plan works for you. It is important to adjust your plan when you need to if you want to lose or maintain weight. Do not worry about making changes to your plan if you do not achieve your required results.

Chapter 13: How to Manage Your Weight Loss

You may have lost a lot of weight throughout your plan and do not want that number to go up. It seems inevitable that you will gain the weight back, but this does not have to be the case if you take care of yourself. An analysis conducted by the National Weight Control Registry showed that it is easy for people to maintain their weight in the long term. The following are some tips you can use to keep losing weight and keep that weight off the scale.

Build Lean Muscle

It is important to maintain your metabolism when you lose weight. You can do this by building lean muscle. Bear in mind that your body has a higher metabolic rate when you have more muscle than fat. If you do not use weights, it is best to add some resistance to your exercise routine now. Doing this will help you increase the weight you work with and challenge yourself.

Eat More Filling Foods

You are bound to feel hungry, but it is important to find a way to keep yourself from eating too much. As mentioned earlier, you can only avoid snacking and binging if you eat full meals. When you increase your fiber and nutrient intake, your hunger will be satiated, and you will not snack every chance you get.

Curb Temptation

Yes, you are not supposed to eat too much of some type of food. This does not mean you should never eat them. You are allowed to give yourself a break every now and then, but it is important never to do it when you are tempted. You can control your weight if you do not give in to your cravings and temptations. It is easy to avoid these temptations by planning your meals ahead, removing any comfort foods or weaknesses from the pantry, and eating out less than you used to.

Count Your Calories

According to the University of Pittsburgh, people lose weight and maintain their weight easily if they watch their caloric intake. You can use a food journal application and make notes about all your meals throughout the day. This helps you track your caloric intake. People are successful at maintaining their weight if they count their calories and limit their intake of fat.

Meal Plans

A weight maintenance diet is like a weight loss diet because you need to plan your meals. If you have a plan ready, it is easy for you to stick to it. Your weight loss plan will have fewer calories when compared to your maintenance plan, but this will keep you on track.

Increase Your Activity Time

Experts recommend that people should exercise for at least 30 minutes every day for at least five days a week. This is only when it comes to losing weight. If you want to maintain your weight, you need to exercise more than you used to. You can walk or perform any activity you like for at least 50 minutes every day if you want to lose weight. You can burn more calories than before and maintain your weight.

Watch Your Portion Sizes

The Centers for Disease Control and Prevention (CDC) conducted a study with 4000 adults as the participants. The research team noted that people who measured their fat and protein intake successfully maintained their weight. This does not mean you have to measure everything you eat, but you should do this at home, so you know how to measure portion sizes if you eat out. It is important to do this so you do not overeat or eat foods that do not help you maintain your weight.

Regular Weighing

It is important to weigh yourself regularly. We have discussed this in detail earlier in the book. If you weigh yourself daily, you will succeed at losing weight and maintaining it. It can be discouraging to weigh yourself regularly if you follow a diet, but this is a great way to maintain your weight.

Eat Dairy

When you eat enough dairy products, specifically low-fat products, you can reduce your hunger pangs. If you crave something sweet, grab a cup of yogurt, and top it with berries. The extra calcium can also improve your bone health, and this is especially important for women.

Use Your Plate as Your Guide

If you cannot measure portions or calculate your caloric intake correctly, use a cup or plate method. This way, you can control your intake. This is a tip commonly used by people on a diet, but it is a great way for you to maintain your weight as well. When you use this method, you need to cover half your plate with vegetables and divide the other half between whole grains and protein. If you do want another helping, swap the whole grains and protein for dairy and fruit.

Stop Watching too much TV

You can maintain your weight easily if you focus on what you are eating. You need to spend time chewing your vegetables and not worrying about why a character on a show wanted revenge.

Chapter 14: Final Push – 21 More Ways to Remain Motivated

This final chapter is just one more set of motivations – things that should give you the push you need to continue on your journey. It will be a long journey, make no mistake about it, but if you are fully prepared mentally, then there will not be a challenge that you cannot overcome.

Think of motivation as being something like the gas you put in your car – the tank doesn't need to be completely full for it to run, but it mustn't be allowed to run empty. Don't ever waste precious time on trying to keep your motivation levels at the maximum because that in itself will wear you down. Motivation has its own natural rhythm – if your motivation levels drop, don't see it as a failure because it isn't.

1. Give it a rest

If your motivation levels start to drop off, take a break from your diet or your fitness regime – just for a period of one to three days, no more. The biggest problem with motivation is that, the more you try catching it, the more elusive it is going to become, so let the natural motivation rhythm run its course. By doing this and by having a plan of habit-changing skills drawn up, you will find it much easier to stay on track, and your motivation levels will simply follow their own natural rhythm

2. Question yourself

When you need a bit of quick inspiration and a bit of a reminder about why you are doing this, ask yourself these questions. Answering them honestly can often be just the boost that you need to carry on:

- What will I look like in six months or a year if I stop my diet?
- How will I feel in six months or a year if I stop my diet?
- What will my health be like if I stop my diet?
- What effect will it have on the people around me – my family, my friends, and myself – if I stop my diet?

Be honest in your answers; if you are not, the only person you are kidding is you.

3. Clean your closet out

If you are finding it tough to stick to your intention to lose weight and get fit, turn to another area of your life. Clean your closet out. Sort out your clothes into those that you will never ever wear again, those that are a size (or two) too small, and those that you wear now. Ditch the clothes you will not wear again, give them to charity, and then look at what is left. Do you want to get into those smaller clothes again or not? Another thing you could do is focus your attention on paying off your debts. The idea is to learn how to stick to a commitment that you have made; if you can do that in one area of your life, you can do it in another, and the sight of those too-small clothes should be just enough motivation to kick you back into gear.

4. Don't keep looking at pictures of models who are super skinny

While it might seem like great inspiration to have pictures of super-skinny models posted everywhere, recent studies have shown that, in fact, the opposite is true. The research involved a group of women who wanted to drop some weight who divided into two groups. Each group was given a food journal to complete – group one had pictures of skinny models on the pages, and group two had a neutral images on theirs. Group two – those with the neutral images – lost weight, whereas the group that had the pictures of the models actually gained weight.

Looking at pictures of these super-thin women is very discouraging for one simple reason – you are creating self-standards that are simply not realistic. If you spend your time looking at a picture of a much thinner woman while you are eating, you are more likely to feel that there is no way on earth you can reach that weight or look, so there isn't any point in trying. Instead of those pictures, look at pictures of you when you were at a good weight and were healthy.

5. Focus on feeling

So many of people focus our entire attention on what number the scale is on and what number they want to reach, or maybe even on the workouts that they have to do to get to that number. That is quite possibly one of the quickest ways to kill off your motivation. Try focusing on something else – how do you feel after you have eaten a wonderful healthy meal or after you finished that last workout? How do you feel when you wake up in the mornings now? Motivation doesn't always have to come first – sometimes, the activity or the feeling you get from that activity can be enough to give you the motivation you need to carry on. Focus on how you are feeling when you finish a run, how many calories you have just burned off, and how good you feel deep inside.

6. Have a "business" plan

All ventures need some kind of plan, especially if they are to be successful. That plan must lay out what the mission or goal is and how you are going to get there. The same goes for when you are looking to lose weight. If you don't have that plan, you don't have the first idea on where you should be starting, where you are heading, or even how you are going to get there.

Your weight loss goal is your business objective. One you know what it is you want to achieve and when you want to achieve it by, then and only then can you begin to work out how you are going to get there. Make sure that your goals are specific and reasonable. It's no good setting goals that are simply not attainable; that's the first step towards failure. Also, don't include any strategies that just won't work, simply because you feel you should.

7. Set a halfway marker

While it is a great idea to give yourself a reward for reaching your goals, it can sometimes take months, even years, to get to a specific point. If you are waiting that long for your rewards, the wind is going to be knocked right out of your sails before you even get your end goal in sight. Instead of waiting to pass the checkered flag at the end, plan a few small treats along the way and something big for the halfway point – something like that cruise you always wanted to do. If you have something like that to look forward to, you are less likely to give up when the going gets tough. I can tell you that it's around that mid-point that things will start to get tough.

8. Act "as if"

Don't wait until you've got that bikini body to take your holiday, go and visit an old friend, or even take up that dance class you've been dreaming of. Do it now; live your life, and enjoy it. Act as though you are already at the weight you want to be at. Think about how you would feel, how you would eat and drink, and what your day would look like. What are you not doing until you reach that weight? Do it now, and move your mind out of punishment mode and into a rewarding mode – one that makes you want to stick at it.

9. Put your motivation on the mirror

I mentioned putting inspirational quotes on your mirror earlier, but you could also go down the route of pinning a photo of you at your best on there or a pair of skinny jeans that you WILL get back into. Pick a special outfit – something that you are really looking forward to putting on – and hang it by your mirror. See yourself wearing it; think about how good it is going to feel to get into it. As it is a photo of you or an item of your clothing, it is a much more realistic goal than pinning those pictures of super-skinny models up.

10. Tough love

Okay, it can be very motivating to see yourself wearing that special outfit, but some people find it even more inspiring and more motivating to imagine how they would be if they did not lose the weight. Ask yourself what life will be like for you in 10 or 20 years if you don't change the path you are travelling. Try to visualize the weight you will be at and the level of fitness you might or might not have, as the case may be. Try to imagine the health conditions that you could have as a result of not making those changes now. Be very honest with yourself here – it's all too easy to say that it'll never happen to you and that everything is just fine. It isn't, or you wouldn't have opted to start your weight loss journey in the first place.

11. Be Competitive

When it comes to shedding ponds, even a small amount of competition can take you a long way. Recent studies have shown that taking part in team-based competitions for losing weight can result in you dropping up to 20% more weight than you would if you were to do it alone. Team captains were shown to lose even more weight than the members of their teams, probably because of the involvement and position they hold in the team. So, if you really want to boost your success rate, get a team together, and head for victory.

12. Why are you really exercising?

The key to maintaining motivation is focusing on what really motivates you to do something. If your family is your inspiration, think about how your diet and exercise plan is going to help you to be around longer for your kids. Then, get your family involved in your plan. Get your partner to come to the gym with you, play physical games with the kids, and get together at the weekend and cook a whole bunch of healthy meals for the week ahead. If you are going to change the patterns of your behavior, you have first got to recognize the patterns and understand why they exist. Once you have done that, your motivation levels can be redirected towards the right areas, and your goal will suddenly seem far more achievable and realistic.

13. A photo a day

A picture really is worth a thousand words sometimes, and in today's age of digital technology and smartphones, it is much easier than it has ever been to build up your own library for personal motivation. Track your progress with a photo app, like Instagram. Post a photo a day, and document all those changes that you probably would not notice otherwise and that scale doesn't always show. You might just be surprised at what you can see in a photo that you didn't see in the mirror.

14. Shut your inner-critic up

We all have that inner critic – the one that criticizes us all the time. That is our bad habit – a way of using self-criticism as a way of trying to motivate ourselves. I've got news for you: It doesn't work. Not only will it not give you any motivation, but it is actually likely to put a serious kink in your efforts as well. When you criticize yourself, what you are doing is engaging a certain part of the brain – the bit that monitors and controls your fight or flight reflex. The result is an increase in the secretion of cortisol, which is a stress hormone, and that, in turn, makes you want foods that are fatty and sweet – comfort foods.

Next time you find yourself in self-critical mode, put your hand over your heart. Hold it there, and breathe in deeply a few times. This changes the psychological state that your mind is in and shuts the negativity down.

15. Have health all around you

Change your home to reflect the new you – the lighter, healthier you. Stock up your fridge with healthy foods, and place prepped foods in clear containers so you can see them. Fill up bowls with fresh fruit, and leave them on the counters. Put all your workout shoes on a nice shoe rack, on display by the front door. Don't leave dirty laundry on your exercise equipment. There is so much you can do to reflect what you want to be that will make it a whole lot easier to follow your plan and stick to it.

16. Use your smartphone

These days, the mobile app stores are packed full of weight loss apps, carb counters, calorie counters, and recipe apps – you name it, and it's there. Picking the right ones to use can mean that you motivation is no more than one tap away. Use the apps to come up with ideas for healthy nutritional meals, to give you the boost you need to get on the way to the gym, or to get some ideas on new exercises. There are plenty to choose from, and you will surely find something that will keep you on the go and moving forward.

17. Write down your personal reasons for losing weight

While we all want to look great in that new outfit or look fit and toned on the beach, sometimes, that just isn't enough motivation to keep you going. Sit down, and write a list of every single reason why you should lose weight. Write down all the things that would be better about you and your life if you weighed less. Perhaps it's feeling a lot healthier, having more confidence, shopping for funky new clothes, or just being able to keep up with your kids – all the things that would be so much easier to do if you just dropped those pounds. Keep your list on hand, and look at it all the time. Remind yourself of why you are doing this and why it's worth sticking to.

18. Recruit some gift givers

It is nice to reward yourself along the way – or at least the thought of it is. Sometimes, the theory is much easier than the practice, and you often become so busy that you simply don't have time to stop and reward yourself. Instead, get your friends involved. Give a few of them $20 to go and buy you a surprise, wrap it up, and give it you. Set the gift giving at certain points – say one gift for every 10 lbs. lost. That is a great way to keep yourself motivated and a nice surprise to look forward to at certain milestones.

19. Set goals that don't rely on the scales

You can do everything right, but sometimes, those scales will just not move, and the weight just does not seem to be shifting as quickly as you would like. Never let that get to you or discourage you. Set other goals – not just a number on the scale. Set little in-between goals, like working out for an extra 10 or 20 minutes a week, running just that bit further, and sticking to your schedule like glue. Then, reward yourself for all of these little goals.

Set goals like staying inside of your calorie range for so many days at a time, for dinking 64 ounces of water a day, or packing up your lunch every day so you don't get tempted by forbidden foods. Celebrating each new goal is a great way to keep your motivation in gear. You may be surprised at how much quicker the weight seems to come off. Do not focus on a number; focus on life instead.

20. Face your fears

Sometimes, it isn't a lack of motivation that gets in your way; it's your fears or your beliefs that are holding you back. Maybe you have been trying to lose weight by exercising but find yourself taking a different route that doesn't go past the gym or not going out for that walk. Ask yourself why this is. Is it because you simply don't want to do the exercise? Is it because you are embarrassed by how you look in your running gear? To get round this, list some alternatives that will keep you on the move, such as doing fitness DVDs at home instead.

21. Cultivate some compassion

If you get to a stage where you feel totally uninspired or are having a down period about what your body looks like, move your focus elsewhere – to some self-appreciation. Don't beat yourself up if you did not reach your goal this week, and instead, be grateful for the fact that you are healthy and that your body can move and do many things for you. Move from thinking about you look to how you feel and function, cultivating a little compassion and gratitude for the body that got you through another week.

Conclusion

Thank you again for purchasing this book!

I hope this book was able to help you to develop a plan to lose weight and maintain your motivation while you work towards your goals.

The next step is to put your plan into action. You can go back to this book anytime you feel down. In times when your motivation dips, you should read the strategies suggested in this book again. This will help you find the best one that is applicable to your situation.

One quote that I did not mention above and one that is very true is "weight loss is NOT a physical challenge; it's a mental one." The determination that you need to succeed and your motivation, inspiration, positivity, strength, enthusiasm, willpower, encouragement, desire, and pride are all determining factors in the success of your weight loss journey, and they all come from within your mind.

Many people believe that losing weight is purely physical, but when you begin to see it as a mental challenge, you will have more chance of success, and you will find it easier to move through that journey. If your mind isn't in gear before you start – if you haven't mentally prepared yourself – it just isn't going to happen.

You must be prepared to do whatever it takes. If you're not, then you're not going anywhere. The only person who can truly motivate you is you. You are the only one who can give yourself the kick you need to carry on, and you are the only one who can truly encourage and cheer yourself as you overcome obstacle after obstacle.

Be warned that the journey to losing weight is not an easy one, and you have to be mentally prepared to do it. Don't expect results overnight because you will be disappointed. It took a long time to add that extra weight to your body, and it's going to take a long while to shift it safely.

Yes, there are plenty of crash diets you can do that will get rid of pounds of fat in a week, but think about this carefully – just how sustainable is that diet? It isn't – I can tell you that now, for free. As soon as you start finding a particular diet difficult to do, you will stop doing it, and you will go straight back to your old ways. Not only will you gain back the weight you lost, but you will most likely gain back a few more pounds as well.

So, learn to take it slow, and trust the process. Your weight loss plan is not a sprint but a marathon. Trust yourself, and focus on doing things that make you happy. Keep yourself active, and eat the right foods so your energy levels do not dip. Use the different applications mentioned in this book to keep yourself on track. Lastly, do not punish yourself for making a mistake. You would not be human if you did not. If you fall off the wagon, get up, brush yourself off, and start again.

If you enjoyed this book, then I'd like to ask you for a favor – would you be kind enough to leave a review for this book on Amazon? It'd be greatly appreciated!

Thank you, and good luck!

FREE E-BOOKS SENT WEEKLY

Resources

https://www.nhs.uk/live-well/healthy-weight/12-tips-to-help-you-lose-weight/

https://www.webmd.com/diet/obesity/features/7-ways-get-your-diet-off-good-start#3

https://www.healthline.com/nutrition/weight-loss-motivation-tips#TOC_TITLE_HDR_18

https://www.shape.com/weight-loss/tips-plans/22-ways-stay-motivated-lose-weight

https://www.healthline.com/nutrition/weight-loss-morning-habits#TOC_TITLE_HDR_11

https://www.self.com/story/small-lifestyle-habits-help-lose-weight

https://denverweightlossclinic.com/6-steps-to-creating-a-customized-diet-plan-for-weight-loss/

https://www.everydayhealth.com/weight/weight-management.aspx

https://pubmed.ncbi.nlm.nih.gov/16339128/

https://pubmed.ncbi.nlm.nih.gov/21852063/

https://www.ncbi.nlm.nih.gov/pmc/articles/PMC3312817/

https://pubmed.ncbi.nlm.nih.gov/22795495/

https://www.makeuseof.com/tag/food-diary-apps/

https://www.ncbi.nlm.nih.gov/pmc/articles/PMC1308011/

https://onlinelibrary.wiley.com/doi/full/10.1111/j.1559-1816.2007.00189.x

https://pubmed.ncbi.nlm.nih.gov/15655039/

https://pubmed.ncbi.nlm.nih.gov/15655039/

https://www.researchgate.net/publication/244890224_Companion_Dogs_as_Weight_Loss_Partners

https://pubmed.ncbi.nlm.nih.gov/16459211/

https://pubmed.ncbi.nlm.nih.gov/25098557/

https://pubmed.ncbi.nlm.nih.gov/26239831/

https://pubmed.ncbi.nlm.nih.gov/16469977/

https://pubmed.ncbi.nlm.nih.gov/14671205/

https://pubmed.ncbi.nlm.nih.gov/18787524/

https://pubmed.ncbi.nlm.nih.gov/25683820/

https://pubmed.ncbi.nlm.nih.gov/21732212/

https://pubmed.ncbi.nlm.nih.gov/25555390/

https://www.ncbi.nlm.nih.gov/pmc/articles/PMC4592764/

https://pubmed.ncbi.nlm.nih.gov/29076610/

https://www.ncbi.nlm.nih.gov/pmc/articles/PMC4138353/

https://pubmed.ncbi.nlm.nih.gov/23332335/

https://www.ncbi.nlm.nih.gov/pmc/articles/PMC4149603/

https://pubmed.ncbi.nlm.nih.gov/23063049/

https://www.ncbi.nlm.nih.gov/pmc/articles/PMC3466912/

https://pubmed.ncbi.nlm.nih.gov/24622804/

https://www.ncbi.nlm.nih.gov/pmc/articles/PMC3973603/

https://pubmed.ncbi.nlm.nih.gov/18198319/

Book 2
Weight Loss

100 Weight Loss Tips

Lose Weight and Maintain Healthy Weight Loss through Diet, Exercise and Lifestyle

3rd Edition

By Nicholas Bjorn

Table of Contents

Introduction

Thank you for choosing my latest book, *"Weight Loss: 100 Weight Loss Tips: Lose Weight and Maintain Healthy Weight Loss through Diet, Exercise and Lifestyle."* With this book, you will learn exactly what you need to start doing today to lose weight and what it takes to reach your weight loss goals.

This book contains proven steps and strategies on how to successfully lose weight. There are a lot of good reasons to lose excess weight. Over the past few years, obesity has become known as the main risk factor for diseases like diabetes and heart ailments. It can also affect your quality of life and prevent you from doing some of the activities that you used to enjoy.

Weight loss can be achieved by changing some aspects of your lifestyle, especially your diet and level of physical activity. This book contains diet, exercise, and lifestyle tips that can motivate you to lose weight. However, you shouldn't stop once you achieve your ideal weight. Maintaining your weight loss also has its own challenges. The last chapter of this book provides some tips on how you can maintain your weight and lose some more.

Thanks again for choosing this book, and I hope you enjoy it!

FREE E-BOOKS SENT WEEKLY

Join North Star Readers Book Club
And Get Exclusive Access To The Latest Kindle Books in Health, Fitness, Weight Loss and Much More...

TO GET YOU STARTED HERE IS YOUR FREE E-BOOK:

Visit to Sign Up Today!
www.northstarreaders.com/weight-loss-kick-start

Chapter 1 – Benefits of Losing Weight

Weight loss is one of the most popular topics in magazines, lifestyle talk shows, and even normal conversation. There are a lot of people who dedicate their lives to helping people achieve their weight goals. Oftentimes, weight loss is considered as the effect of pop culture and social media, which cultivate images of the "perfect" body. However, losing weight has a lot of short-term and long-term benefits. These benefits are definitely worth the patience and hard work necessary to lose weight.

1. Diabetes and Prediabetes Prevention

Prediabetes occurs when the body has blood glucose that is higher than normal but not high enough to be diagnosed as diabetes. Type 2 diabetes occurs when the body doesn't produce enough insulin to function properly. Having prediabetes can place a person at a higher risk of developing diabetes in the future.

Obesity is one of the major risk factors of type 2 diabetes. It can be difficult for the body's cells to respond to insulin if it carries excess weight. Fat cells act like a wall that prevents sugar from entering the cells, thus resulting in a higher blood sugar level. Studies show that even just a weight loss of 7% through a combination of diet and exercise can prevent prediabetes by 60%.

2. Makes You Heart Healthy

The major risk factors of heart disease are high cholesterol and high blood pressure. Accumulation of excess body fat can cause blood pressure to increase and can trigger the liver to produce high amounts of cholesterol. Losing weight will reduce your blood pressure, along with reducing the amount of cholesterol in your body.

3. Improved Sleep by Reducing Snoring

Snoring happens when the airways are constricted, consequently producing the basic characteristics of a "snore." People who carry excess weight tend to have excess tissue in their neck. This excess tissue increases the chances of snoring and can also lead to a serious and life-threatening condition known as sleep apnea. This condition occurs when the airway is obstructed and the person has to wake up to breathe again. Losing weight reduces the total amount of fat in the body, including that in the neck. Maintaining a healthy weight also improves sleep quality. People who are fit and slim sleep well and have deeper sleep and a wonderful sleep cycle. Such people also have less nightmares, and they wake up feeling refreshed.

4. Pain-free Joints

Excess weight can place strain on your joints, which consequently become swollen and tender. Movement can be very difficult if you have a joint disorder. Even a weight loss of 5% of your total body weight can significantly reduce the amount of stress on your hips, knees, and back. Weight loss can also increase your standing time, as you can stand for longer times if you lose weight. This is great for teachers and professors who are supposed to stand up a lot. It won't have much of a negative effect.

5. Improved Energy

Losing weight through regular exercise can enhance your strength and vitality. Moderate workouts in the morning can help keep you energized throughout the day. This is a great benefit for people who often find themselves sleepy after lunch. Weight loss makes you highly active as well. You feel fresh, active, and peppy throughout the day. You can finish heavy tasks in less time without feeling tired. A sort of different aura will surround you, which will also make you appear more positive and radiant because of weight loss.

6. You Feel Better

Losing weight can naturally make you feel better. The extra weight that you carry in your stomach can squeeze the kidney and prevent it from processing toxins, which can make you feel sluggish. You will also feel lighter and more confident. Exercise releases hormones that are responsible for making you feel good. Losing weight and achieving a healthy body can also boost your self-confidence. You will start to realize that you are capable of accomplishing your goals, which will make you feel more confident about your skills. All of this happens because subconsciously people develop a negative image of themselves when they are overweight. Partly, society is to blame for this. However, when you lose weight, you definitely start feeling more confident and attractive. Use this new power to keep yourself well maintained and to prevent the weight and fats from coming back.

Chapter 2 – 40 Diet Tips to Lose Weight

Watching what you eat is one of the best ways to successfully lose weight. Dieting has become very popular recently and still is gaining a lot of popularity. However, not all diets are healthy; some of them are actually fad diets that may help you lose weight in less time, but these diets will actually cause more problems than benefits. These diets are famous for quick weight loss, so people tend to ignore their side effects. Unfortunately, some of the side effects of such diets can actually prove to be fatal. Weight loss is important but not more important than your life; do not forget that.

However, the above statement does not mean that you cannot use dieting to lose weight–you surely can–but instead of relying on fad diets or crash diets, you should ideally consult you GP or a good dietician who can help you to formulate a good diet plan according to your body and health. If you do not want to go to a doctor or a dietician, you can always find some really great diet options online, but remember not to look for fad or crash diets. Weight loss is supposed to be a long process because sudden weight loss may actually cause many problems.

Here are some foods and diet tips that can help you lose weight.

1. Create a Grocery List

Eating healthy is a very crucial part of the weight loss process. You have to keep this in mind and stock up on healthy food accordingly. You cannot pick up random foods from the grocery aisles anymore. Make a grocery list before you visit the store. This will allow you to stay on track and help you avoid any unhealthy purchases. You have to make conscious choices about what you eat if you want to lose weight.

A grocery list will help you with this. We all tend to prepare our meals with whatever is at hand at home. This means that you will be preparing healthy meals if you stock up on healthy ingredients. However, if you buy bags of chips and cookies, you will most likely be reaching for them at some point in the day.

Instead, you can create a grocery list that includes nutrient-rich food that will benefit your body, and only buy these on your next grocery store run. Instead of sugar-laden cookies, add some whole grain crackers to your list. These kinds of switches in your grocery list will make a lot of difference in what you consume in the long run. Buy nutritious foods that will fit into your weight loss plan.

The following are some of the foods you should include in your healthy grocery list:

- Whole grains like brown rice, buckwheat groats, whole-wheat pasta or tortillas, and whole grain bread.
- Fruits like papaya, kiwi, cantaloupe, strawberries, blueberries, avocado, oranges, apples, bananas, honeydew melon, and grapes.
- Vegetables like acorn squash, spinach, Swiss chard, red peppers, red lettuce, tomatoes, onions, broccoli, garlic, ginger, lemons, cilantro, and carrots.
- Beans and legumes like pinto beans, white beans, green beans, and garbanzo beans.
- Fish like salmon, king mackerel, trout, and Bluefin tuna.

- Dairy and soy foods like nonfat milk, soy yogurt, reduced-fat cheddar cheese, soy turkey, soy cheese, soybeans, and eggs.

- Nuts, seeds, and foods like olive oil, almonds, tahini, and walnuts.

- Condiments like salt, pepper, ground cumin, Italian dressing, maple syrup, vegetable broth, chicken broth, balsamic vinegar, red wine vinegar, cinnamon, honey mustard, salsa, and cornstarch.

All of the above are foods that usually fit into any healthy diet. So, the next time you grab a cart at the grocery store, stick to foods that are only included in your list. Avoid loading up on anything that you will feel guilty about eating later.

Meal planning is a great idea when you want to have greater control over your diet. It involves planning out all your meals for a week or more. Then, you can prepare most of the ingredients and even prepare the food and keep it ready for consumption. The dishes will be portioned out so that you have food ready for all your meals. Some of the dishes can be half-cooked, or you can just keep the ingredients ready for you to cook when you actually want to eat. The point is that you can start meal prepping to help you with weight loss. While you decide on the dishes you want for the week, check out the recipes that are given later in the book. It will give you an idea about the kind of food you can eat while trying to lose weight.

Recipes will have ingredient lists, and these can be of great help. Note down all the ingredients you will require to prepare all the food. This will be your weekly grocery list. You can mindfully buy things that you will be using during the week while staying away from other potentially fattening food. This will save you a lot of time and serve as another great way to do better on your weight loss plan.

You can keep trying new dishes that are suitable for your goals while enjoying your food without worrying about gaining weight. A thorough grocery list before you go shopping will save you a lot of stress and time for the next week or so. Everything you need and should be eating will be stocked up in the house. Remember to get rid of the unhealthy food in your pantry that might set you adrift from your goals.

2. Shop the Perimeter of the Grocery Store

Even when you go to the grocery store, there is a right way and a wrong way to be shopping. Most of us mindlessly wander around the grocery store and pick up whatever we want. It has also been noticed that people have a tendency to shop more from the aisles in the center. If you think about it, you will usually walk straight into the center when you enter a store. However, if you want to eat healthier, you should be shopping at the perimeters of your local grocery store. Typically, the healthiest foods are at the back or the outer sides of the grocery store.

Most of the fresh food will be stocked in this area. Fresh foods like produce, dairy, or meat are generally kept in the perimeter region of most grocery stores and should be what you buy more of. These foods are much healthier than the processed foods that you generally buy from the center aisles. The center aisles are stocked to the brim with tons of options, but all of this is processed and unhealthy food. You don't need to buy varieties of cookies and chips just because they taste good and there are always new flavors to try.

The modern diet is filled with this kind of junk food, and this is why most of us suffer from weight issues. The availability of these processed foods has made things a lot more convenient, but this comes at the cost of our health. Buying fresh produce is always the better choice, even if it takes up time to cook your own meals. It allows you to have a lot more control over how much fat and sodium you consume in your diet. It is important for you to take notice of what is added to your food if you want to maintain a healthy diet.

Processed foods usually have a lot of preservatives that do more harm and good in the long run. Such ingredients allow manufacturers to increase the shelf life of their food products. However, there are chemicals and hidden additives that have a negative effect on your body. A packet of chips can lie on the shelf for months together, while fruits and vegetables have to be switched out every few days.

In their natural state and without preservatives, food tends to spoil quite easily. However, these wholesome fresh foods are what your body needs. You need to fill your kitchen with baskets of fresh fruits, and the fridge should only have vegetables and fresh meat. The processed meals and condiments have minimal nutrition and a ton of calories to add to your weight. So, opt for as much of the fresh foods from the perimeters as possible, and avoid the central aisles when you go grocery shopping again. The added benefit is that you will also be saving a lot of money while you do this.

3. Include Whole Foods, and Cut Down on Processed Foods

Like we mentioned above, it is important to eat more whole foods and less processed foods. A diet that is rich in whole foods is more likely to help you lose weight over time. This is because whole foods are usually much closer to their natural state than any processed food.

Processed foods will have a lot of additives, such as sugar, salt, starch, flavorings, and other things that will actually cause an increase in weight and even harm your health. They have certain substances that allow manufacturers to keep them on the shelves longer, but these substances are harmful to the human body. Whole foods are more nutritious and allow you to eat clean. They won't have hidden ingredients that you have to worry about. Eating whole foods gives you more control over what you put in your body.

For instance, opt for potatoes from the produce section, and avoid buying potato chips from processed foods. Buy a whole chicken, and grill it for lunch instead of eating chicken nuggets. Check the labels of the foods you purchase, and avoid foods that are overly processed. They will be filled with preservatives and artificial ingredients while barely providing any nutrition. You might be a little unsure about what is processed and what is considered a whole food, so the following should help you out:

- Whole foods include fresh fruits, vegetables, milk, nuts, seeds, meat, poultry, beans, and seafood.
- Processed foods include ready-to-eat meals, refined carbohydrates, foods that have added sugars, junk food, and anything that is highly processed.

When you are buying fruits and vegetables, try to get the freshest variety. Canned or frozen foods should be consumed only if there are minimal additives added. Packaged fruit juices are processed and usually filled with sugars, but making juice from the real fruit will be a wholesome option. It would also be a better option to soak beans at home before preparing them instead of buying canned beans.

Milk itself is a whole food, but dairy products are processed to a certain level. Buy minimally processed cheese and yogurt. Be careful about the meat or poultry you buy as well because some varieties contain a lot of hormones and antibiotics that you should preferably avoid. Ready-to-eat foods may save you time, but they are not healthy and cause weight gain. Prepare meals from scratch for better nutrition and taste. Foods with refined carbohydrates are processed and should be avoided. This includes puffed rice and anything that is made from white flour.

When grains are ground into flour, they become more glycemic. Opt for barley, quinoa, or brown rice.

4. Curb Your Sweet Tooth Naturally

Sweet treats like candies, cakes, and cookies are very delicious and appetizing, but they are loaded with artificial ingredients that do not provide much benefit for the body. Additionally, these sugary foods can have negative effects on the body. These treats have high calories and thus make it easier for you to gain weight. They can also trigger blood sugar fluctuations that can cause mood swings.

However, it is also unrealistic and unreasonable to remove all sweet foods from your diet completely. Fruits are called "nature's candy" because of their natural sweetness. Unlike candies, fruits contain fiber, vitamins, and minerals that can provide many benefits for the body. Keep a stash of fruit in your kitchen so that you won't be tempted to overindulge in processed sweets when you have a craving.

5. Slow Down and Hara Hachi Bu Rule

It takes about 20 minutes for the body to realize that you are already full. Eating mindlessly can make you eat more calories than you need. Take time to enjoy your meals. It is better if you eat on a table instead of in front of the television because watching can distract you from enjoying your meal. Take your time, and eat slowly. A study at the University of Rhode Island showed that a person can lose about 2 pounds a month if they eat slowly because they become more aware of what they are consuming.

You should also avoid eating too much food until you are stuffed full. Overeating can make it uncomfortable for you to move or even breathe afterwards. There is a practice in Japan known as "hara hachi bu" where you should eat only until you feel that you are 80% full. Do undertake this practice, and avoid eating until you get full. According some Indian traditions, you should divide your stomach into three parts. So, fill half of your stomach with food, a quarter with water, and a quarter with air.

6. Do Not Completely Eliminate Carbohydrates

Carbohydrates have been labeled as one of the causes of weight gain. However, the real reason behind its bad reputation is that most of the carbohydrates that people consume are highly processed. If a standard diet of eating processed carbs and one that is low in carbohydrates are compared, it looks like the latter wins in terms of being the best way to lose weight. However, the results are different if the low-carbohydrate diet is compared with a good carb diet that is low in processed foods and sugars.

Before 1991, Japanese people made carbohydrates part of their regular meals. They often eat rice and sweet potatoes, but they are considered one of the healthiest people in the world. Obesity is uncommon in Japan, unlike the case in other countries. The body needs adequate carbohydrates to function well. Completely removing carbohydrates from your diet can affect the hormones responsible for fat loss and consequently make it harder for you to lose weight. As a general rule, eat more carbohydrates on days in which you expect to be more physically active.

7. Increase Consumption of Fruits and Vegetables

People who eat more fruits and vegetables are healthier and slimmer than those who constantly eat processed foods. Fruits and vegetables are rich in nutrients that can give you energy. Moreover, these foods are free from sugars and artificial ingredients, which can be toxic to the body. Aim to eat different colored vegetables and fruits. Fortunately, fruits and vegetables are delicious and versatile, so you can add them to your dishes easily.

8. Choose Grilled Food over Fried

The way you cook your food will have a big impact on the quality of your diet and its effect on your weight loss plan. It is a healthier option to grill food than fry them. Frying involves a lot of oil or fat, and this can cause weight gain. It may be tempting to eat such fried foods because they taste and smell good, but they are not going to help you lose weight. Instead, you can switch over to grilling most of the foods that you usually fry. They will taste good, and you will also have the satisfaction of knowing that you are eating healthy.

Fried foods cause high calorie intake, and it results in unwanted weight gain. If you opt to cook most of your food by frying, it will be more difficult to manage your weight. In fact, a lot of nutrition is lost from certain foods when they are fried. The high temperature of the fat or oil that you fry the food with will result in moisture loss and will cause vitamins to be eliminated. Fried foods are also much harder to digest than grilled foods. You need to eat food that can be digested well and not stored as fat.

Any food that has a very high fat content will exert too much pressure on your digestive system and can cause health issues. Grilling is a healthier cooking method with many benefits. When you grill meat, it will have reduced fat when you eat it. This is because a lot of fat will melt off the meat while grilling. It will allow you to consume a diet that is much lower in fat content. The calorie content of grilled food is also lower than that of fried food. Your calorie consumption will be much more controlled, and this will promote better weight management.

Eating more grilled food will also help you achieve lower levels of bad cholesterol in your body. Fried food increases bad cholesterol and affects cardiovascular health. Changing your method of cooking will reduce your risk of developing conditions like type 2 diabetes, stroke, high blood pressure, etc. Grilling will ensure that your food is much more nutritious, thus improving your overall health while helping you lose excess weight. It will prevent moisture loss from your food and also retain the vitamins you need.

Many people don't know that grilling food allows vegetables to retain more vitamins and minerals than frying does. Grilling is especially better for vegetables that already have low water content because it allows them to retain moisture. Another advantage is that the vegetables that are usually chosen for grilling are fresh and in season. This is a better alternative to canned veggies and will aid in your weight loss plan.

When you grill a slab of meat over a fire, it will preserve more of its thiamine and riboflavin. These have their own health benefits and play a vital role in the diet. Once you master the process of grilling your food, you will always opt for it over frying. Given that grilled food retains more moisture, you will also be less inclined to add any fattening condiments like butter to your food. This means that your meals will have fewer calories. Opt for lean meats to grill because they will give you more protein and less fat. No matter what you cook, grilling is the way to do it. Healthy cooking will contribute to better weight management.

9. Increase Fiber Intake

Increasing your fiber intake can encourage weight loss by making you feel full even if you consume fewer calories. Eating fiber-rich foods like whole grains, whole produce, and beans can also reduce your cravings, making you less likely to binge on unhealthy foods later in the day.

10. Be Conscious of Your Calorie Intake

Consuming fewer calories than what you burn is the most straightforward way to lose weight. Your ideal calorie intake depends on your current weight, height, and level of physical activity. There are calorie calculators online that automatically calculate these numbers. You can easily reduce your calorie intake by consuming less processed food and focusing on nourishing your body with whole food. However, you should also refrain from eating very few calories because this can be detrimental to your health. As you lose weight, you should adjust your calorie budget accordingly because you will need fewer calories as your body becomes lighter.

11. Increase Water Intake

Drinking water has numerous benefits, including detoxification and suppressing your appetite. There are times when you confuse thirst for hunger. Drinking water can help you reduce your food intake and make you feel fuller. It also reduces water retention in the body, which can help you lose a lot of water weight. Water should be your choice of beverage rather than high-calorie sodas and juices.

12. Use Your Utensils Carefully

You can eat less by using different utensils and plates when eating. By simply using a smaller plate, you can trick your brain into thinking that you are consuming more food. This rule also applies to drinks. Tall and lean drinking glasses are better than short and wide ones. Some people also opt to use chopsticks instead of a spoon and fork to help them eat more slowly.

13. Have Occasional Treats

Having the perfect diet that eliminates all kinds of unhealthy food is unrealistic. Aiming for perfection can be counterproductive because it can make you feel deprived and depressed. It is okay to indulge in your favorite treats every once in a while. A few scoops of ice cream and one slice of cake will not hurt your diet. However, be careful not to make these occasional treats a regular indulgence. Aim to have treats comprise 10% to 15% of your total diet. This way, you will not feel deprived.

14. Learn to Cook Delicious Food and Invest in Equipment

Relying on restaurant food can be detrimental to your health and budget. Invest in a good cookbook, and start cooking on your own. Learning how to cook can be fun and exciting. You will also feel a sense of accomplishment after preparing dishes that you and your family can enjoy. Cooking your own food can enable you to control your ingredients and serving sizes.

You should also invest in kitchen equipment to make cooking easier. If you often lack time to cook at home, you can purchase a slow cooker so that you can simply prepare the ingredients ahead of time and come home to a warm cooked meal in the evening. A slow cooker is also very versatile and economical because it consumes less electricity than an oven.

A food processor and blender are also great tools to use. You can make fruit shakes and green smoothies using a blender. Such shakes and smoothies are great alternatives to whole vegetables and fruits. Finally, store your leftovers in the freezer after cooking a large batch of food. Freezing the food can maintain freshness and preserve nutrients. You can also buy a large bulk of fresh vegetables and fruits that are on sale and then freeze them to prolong their shelf life.

15. Plan Out and Shop for Snacks

A properly devised and developed exercise and diet routine is extremely essential for anyone who wants to lose weight. Without a proper plan, your hard work may not benefit you at all. Everyone loves snacks, and people who love food are generally reluctant about dropping their favorite snacks. Unfortunately, most of these generally loved snacks are fatty and unhealthy. However, you do not need to drop your snacks altogether; you just need to reduce your intake of these snacks. It is also advisable to plan out your snacks once a week. This preplanning is always helpful and will prevent binge eating or unhealthy eating.

16. Healthy Recipes

Generally, everyone loves food but more often than not, all of us love foods that are considered to be fatty and very unhealthy. Instead of eating these fatty and unhealthy foods, you should opt for healthy and nutritious foods. It is a very popular myth that healthy and nutritious food does not taste good. This is a lie. Nutritious and healthy food can be very tasty if you follow good and well-tested recipes. You can find such recipes online. These recipes will make you fall in love with healthy food. You can also buy recipe books that are specially made for people who want to lose weight. These recipes are well researched so they will not have any side effects.

If you have some health problems, you should ideally consult with your dietician or doctor first about recipes. Your dietician can prescribe and suggest the best recipes for you.

17. Distinct Journals

In the next few chapters, you will find that I have mentioned a lot about keeping journals. Keeping at least two journals concerning your diet is highly necessary. The personal journal will be explained in the next chapters, but here, we will talk about the public journal. Keeping a public journal that you can share with the public or friends is a very good way to keep yourself motivated. As the public will check your progress every day, you will feel a sense of responsibility, as well as a challenge to do well. This responsibility and challenge will lead you to results faster.

You can keep a public journal in many ways, of which two are extremely common and easy to do. You can send an e-copy of your journal every night to your friends through email. Another option is posting your progress in online forums for weight loss. These two options will help you a lot. You should always keep one thing in mind though; you should always fill in correct details and information in your journal, as wrong information can ruin your diet plan. Remember, honesty is the best policy for losing weight.

18. Jot it Down

Keep a big white board or chalkboard in your kitchen, and jot down your total diet plan on this board. Jotting down your diet plan and keeping it in focus all the time will keep you motivated and accountable. This constant reminder will keep you active and peppy. You should also jot down your weekly meal plan on the board so that you can follow the plan thoroughly. By making a weekly plan, you can keep a track of your daily calories and nutrients easily.

Another benefit of keeping a white board or chalkboard is that you can write beautiful inspirational and motivational quotes on it. Although motivational quotes have faced a lot of ridicule in recent times, this does not mean they are useless. You can feel the change if you keep yourself motivated. Remember, losing weight is not just about physical strength; it is also about mental strength and mind power. If you keep yourself motivated, the journey of weight loss will not be hard at all.

19. Curb Those Cravings

One of the biggest if not ***the*** biggest enemy of your weight loss journey is craving. Human beings are heavy gluttons—we love food. It's not a hyperbole if someone says that we live to eat not eat to live. Unfortunately, diet is all about controlling your intake of calories, which means controlling your intake of food as well. However, as human beings, we cannot control ourselves when we are on restrictions to eat food.

Curbing the cravings is not much of an issue if you are full all the time. This can be achieved by eating foods that are rich in fiber and are filling. Another major problem with cravings is that sometimes you get cravings even when you are full. You need to understand that these cravings are not actually cravings but just boredom or emotional pain. People eat food when they feel sad, frustrated, angry, or even when they are bored. To overcome these cravings, you should try doing things that will kill your boredom or will help you to overcome your pain, sadness, depression, tension, anger, etc. These activities may include chatting with a close friend, going out for a walk, taking a bath, sleeping, reading your favorite book, etc. Doing yoga and some breathing exercises are also good options.

20. Be Prepared, Be Ready

Hunger can strike anytime, anywhere. It is highly necessary to address your cravings effectively. You should not eat high fatty foods etc to curb your cravings. You should ideally keep cut fruits and veggies in your refrigerator for emergency cravings. Cut-up fruits and veggies are not only effective in curbing the cravings, but you can also arrange a quick snack or cook a small but healthy meal instantly with these sliced and diced veggies and fruits.

21. Throw Away the Junk

It has already been established that human beings love food, especially junk food. Keeping junk food in the house, especially in places that can be reached easily, is a massive problem. You keep on going back to your junk food because human beings simply cannot control their desires for too long if their prey sits smugly in front of them. We succumb to such desires, which are quite natural, but this should be avoided at all costs.

To overcome this problem, it is advisable to throw out all the junk food from your house. Now, this is quite easy if you are a bachelor or spinster, but it might become a nuisance for people who have roommates or live with their family, partner, spouse, etc. For such people, the only option is to make the others understand that snacking can be a very big hindrance to your diet and exercise regime, and so to help you, they should keep off the snacks for a bit. If this does not work (and there are a lot of chances of this happening), you can try asking them to buy small amounts of snacks at a time, which can be eaten in one go or, at most, two go's. This will definitely help you avoid snacks.

22. Low-calorie Meals and Tasty Smoothies

This tip might be very hard to follow as people love to eat, as already established in this book a few times. Reducing your meal to such a simple affair of 300 to 400 calories is a hard thing to do, especially if you are accustomed to heavy meals and unhealthy foods. You will probably feel irritated, frustrated, and sometimes downright angry if you simply try to shift to a diet with meals consisting of just 300 to 400 calories. You can obviously tolerate this kind of diet and prevent these sorts of side effects if you plan your diet properly. Instead of eating 40 calories of ice cream or something of that sort, you should concentrate hard on including foodstuffs that are low on calories but still highly fulfilling. These things will help you feel satiated quite easily and quickly without consuming a lot of calories. Moreover, these calories are not the so-called empty calories.

There are certain options that are supposed to be really fulfilling as well. These options include healthy and tasty smoothies. You can make tasty smoothies and add healthy ingredients, such as avocados, greens, berries, etc. These things will revamp your smoothies and will make them even more healthy and delicious.

Remember, 300 to 400 calories do not have to be a bad thing if you manage your diet well. You will get so accustomed to this diet in no time, such that you will not want to go back to your normal diet ever.

23. Never Skip Breakfast

It is believed that breakfast is known as ***break-fast*** because you literally break the night-long fast with some food in the morning. This simple myth—or fact—talks about the importance of this meal. Breakfast is definitely the most important meal of the day. There is a famous saying that goes: “Have breakfast like a king, lunch like a minister, and dinner like a pauper.” This definitely shows why you should always eat a large breakfast. You can actually consume high amounts of calories during breakfast. By high, we mean high but still at a healthy level. You can eat a heavy breakfast because most of the calories gained from breakfast are lost throughout the day, and if you work out or even go for a simple walk, you will not put on weight at all.

Breakfast can include anything, but ideally, you should eat something that is not exactly heavy but is, at least, fulfilling so that your hunger will be curbed, and you will feel satiated for a long time. According to research, it is believed that you should not just eat your breakfast but you should actually eat it as soon as you wake up—specifically, within an hour of you waking up. This is supposed to enhance your metabolism and keep you motivated and active. An active and fast-working metabolism is highly essential for fast weight loss.

24. Eat This, Not That

Ghrelin is a hormone in our body that is responsible for stimulating our appetite and making us hungry. This hormone is quite important and necessary, but it can cause problems while losing weight because it will keep on making you hungry. You can suppress this hormone by doing one easy thing, which is adding around 10 to 15 grams of protein to your diet every day. You can add this protein in any way or form, but natural proteins derived from food items are always a better option. You can try adding eggs to your diet. Eggs are not only satiating, but they are also a rich source of protein, so they can actually curb your hunger.

With this, you should also try and include at least 10 grams of fiber to your diet every day. Again, this fiber can be of any kind but natural food-derived fiber is always a better option. You can also get a good amount of fiber from flaxseeds, psyllium husks, etc. Fiber is important because it satiates hunger for a long duration and can also prevent bloating, which is a common symptom of constipation. Remember to drink lots of water when you are consuming a lot of fiber.

Going low carb is an essential thing to lose weight. However, limiting all the carbs will not help you. You should try and limit carbs, such as refined carbs, which you get from muffins and bagels, and instead, you should add a small amount of good fats.

25. Measure Up!

Measuring your daily food proportions is not only a great habit while losing weight, but it is also a great thing if you want to maintain your weight. Ideally, you should not rely on simple bowls and your eyesight for measuring the portions, as these two things can betray you. Instead of relying on these things, you should buy and use good quality measuring spoons and cups. You can measure a lot of things using these cups and spoons, such as cereal, fruits, oatmeal, meal, nuts, yogurt, etc. You can also buy a small kitchen-level weighing machine, which will not only help you in measuring things for your weight loss but will also help you in baking, etc.

26. Breakfast Made Healthy

We have already covered breakfast and its importance in a previous tip. A lot of people ask how they can make a good, healthy, and fulfilling breakfast that can keep them satiated for a long time without causing any problems. You can do this in a lot of ways, and here, we highlight three really good ones. You can make and bake some healthy scones, cakes, etc., that you can consume whenever you want to have a quick yet healthy breakfast. Ideally, you should keep such things ready all the time so as to avoid a quick snack from a shop or bakery because these snacks are, more often than not, full of calories and unhealthy carbs and fats. You can also try baking the things that you normally fry or deep fry. They might not taste as good as the fried versions, but they will definitely remove a lot of calories from your diet.

While making pancakes, you should use wholegrain flour or other kinds of healthy flour. To make the pancakes healthier, you should experiment with them. You can try adding mashed, baked, or boiled sweet potatoes to the pancakes. You can also try adding blueberries, mashed spinach, and pureed greens, etc., which can increase the nutritive value of your breakfast. Quacked quinoa is also a great option.

Instead of drinking fruit juices, etc., you should try and eat the original fruits. These fruits contain fiber, which is lost when you make juices out of them. Fruits, such as grapefruit, are highly rich in fiber and should ideally be consumed all the time instead of making juice out of it.

27. Healthy Soup and Preparation of the Day

Everyone loves a hot meal. The heat makes the meal tastier and more delicious as well. However, in today's modern world, making a hot, tasty, and healthy meal every day is not always possible. You should not use these ready-to-cook meals that are packed with empty calories. Instead, to eat a hot meal every day, you can try making a huge pot full of vegetable bean soup. Then, you could divide this soup in two or more cup containers and then store them in the freezer. When you want to eat a hot meal, just take this container out of the freezer and thaw it until it gets to room temperature. Heat it over medium heat in a pot and then enjoy this delicious meal.

28. Cut the Calories

Here are some simple ways to reduce calories:

- Do not buy boxes and packs of snacks from stores. These packs more often than not contain large amounts of unhealthy ingredients that are very bad for your health. Instead of relying on these products, you should ideally buy small empty containers and then fill them with fruits and healthy snacks for you to eat at the office, school, etc.

- Although this tip might seem to be overkill, you should ideally count and label calories on each food item in your house. This will help you to keep track of your food and eating habits. It will also help you avoid over indulging and overeating. It will also become very easy for you to keep track of your diet, such that maintaining a journal will become a very easy task for you.

- Salads are very healthy, even if they are frozen. Unfortunately, the salads available outside are often very unhealthy and fattening. It is believed that salads from fast food chains are even unhealthier than the fast food options available in these chains. You should not rely on the salads available outside, and instead, you should make your own salads. You should prepare a large amount of salad on Sunday. You can then pack the salad in five to six containers and then freeze them. You can then eat these salads every day by thawing them to room temperature.

- To make your salads even healthier, you should think of adding whole grains, corn, sprouts, etc., to them. By adding these things, you can get the best of both worlds and have a lot of nutrients together. These grains and sprouts will also help you to feel satiated and will prevent hunger for a long time. You can boil the grains and sprouts, but ideally, you should have the sprouts raw.

- If you are a sandwich lover, you should always use brown bread instead of the plain white bread. Instead of using wrap, you should use Swiss chard leaves or spinach. Cheese should be altogether skipped, or you should try to find an alternative that is healthier than regular cheese. You should add a lot of veggies to your sandwich.
- Avoid soda, soft drinks, etc., at all costs. Ideally, you should also stop consuming alcohol. Instead of consuming soda, soft drinks, iced tea, cold coffee, etc., you should add green tea, lavender tea, water, sugarless lemonade, etc., to your diet. Although these things are not that tasty, they are very healthy. Green tea is actually supposed to help you burn those calories.
- Avoid cream cheese at all costs. Instead, use peanut butter or almond butter, and spread it on your food items instead of cream cheese or simple butter. Healthy fats not only help to satiate you, but they also help curb your hunger and can even decrease your belly fats.

29. Swap It!

You can swap a lot of things in your diet that you love but are unhealthy with healthy things that taste great as well. This swapping will help you to control your hunger and will make you eat healthy stuff as well. This will also prevent you from eating unhealthy food items. You can use the following tips to learn swapping:

- Instead of eating ice cream, you should try a healthy alternative that tastes nearly the same as ice cream but is way healthier: Blend frozen bananas, peanut butter, cherries, etc., together, and then freeze this mixture. Serve this mixture as an ice cream. You can also top it with a couple of nuts.

- Instead of using spaghetti, use long juliennes of carrots, zucchini, etc. They obviously won't taste like the pasta, but they are definitely healthier.

- Instead of using fatty dips and spreads like mayonnaise, use healthy spreads like hummus, mustard, puree of roasted red pepper, and seasoned tomato puree.

- Instead of eating potato chips, try eating baked carrot chips. You can also try eating baked potato chips, but ideally, you should not eat a lot of potatoes.

- If you are making a dish that needs cream, you can try replacing it with silken tofu. You obviously cannot replace cream in all the recipes, but in some recipes, such as dairy-free chocolate mousse, it can work wonders.

- Use skimmed milk instead of full fat milk, and if you already use skimmed milk, then move over to almond milk instead.

- Instead of using white bread, always use brown bread, or use a wrap.

30. Desserts and How to Make Them Healthy

Cutting out sugar is a major part of nearly every diet in existence. Unfortunately, we love sugar, and cravings for sugar definitely are the strongest. Desserts are the most missed things on a diet. However, no need to worry; below are some of the major tips that can help you to cut out the sugar but still be able to eat desserts as well.

- Instead of dying a little daily in the memory of food and desserts, you should actually eat a small amount of sweet things every day. This will help you keep your mind calm and fresh, and you won't find yourself pining for a bowl of ice cream afterwards.

- Instead of using artificial sweeteners or sugar while making desserts, you should try adding fruits and natural sweeteners instead. You can make healthy cakes and muffins with these fruits and natural sweetener.

- You should also try adding vegetables to baked goods. These vegetables can be of any kind. You can add zucchini, carrots, sweet potatoes, etc., to your muffins and cakes. Normally, you won't be able to taste these things, and you will actually consume a lot of nutrients without even getting a taste of the veggies.

- You can also try adding natural protein powders to your desserts to make them healthier.

- You can replace your dessert with a bowl of healthy yogurt or low-fat and low-calorie smoothies. These will also help you remain satiated.

31. Snacks and How to make them Healthy

After desserts, snacks are definitely the most missed things when you are on a diet. However, you do not need to cut your snacks, which we have already established. Here, you will find some great tips to make your snacks healthier and your snack times better.

- It is necessary to limit your snack to around 150 calories only. You should avoid eating snacks that have more calories than this amount. You should ideally add a lot of fiber to your snacks. Some healthy snacks include fruits, seeds, etc. Remember, portions are very important.

- Instead of eating sugars, you should try to eat proteins. Proteins will not cause you to crash as they are high sources of energy. Prolonging your meal or snack is also an effective way of eating less. You can do this by consuming food that takes a lot of time to eat. For instance, you can try snacking on pods of edamame. These pods need a lot of time to eat and, thus, are a great way to prolong your meal. These pods are also high in protein and are supposed to be one of the richest protein sources. You can get around 12 grams of proteins from a single cup serving of these pods.

- Always carry your own snacks. They might seem to be a nuisance, but they can actually help you to avoid unhealthy snacks from stores, bakeries, fast-food chains, food joints, etc. Not only will this keep you on your diet, but it is also very good in keeping you from spending a lot of money on empty calories.

- Wet snacks are a better option if you are in house. Wet snacks contain a lot of water, and this will help you get full faster and will prevent bloating as well. Wet snacks commonly include melons, cherries, tomatoes, cherry tomatoes, pepper, celery, etc.
- Sprouts are also a good option for snacks. You can always eat a bowl full of sprouts to curb your hunger.
- An apple a day keeps the doctor away. Also, an apple a day will help you keep hunger at bay. Apples are full of fiber, and they have natural appetite suppressants. By eating an apple daily, you can effectively suppress your appetite.

32. Reduce the Size of Your Plate

We use dinner plates for eating our dinner, which is not a ridiculous thing at all. However, instead of using dinner plates, you should try and use salad plates for meals instead. It is believed that if you use small plates, you actually feel satiated early and do not overeat. This will definitely help you stick to your diet plan.

33. Chewing Gum All the Time

We tend to eat a lot and snack a lot if we do not have anything in our mouth. This particularly happens when a person is cooking. You can prevent this from happening if you chew gum while cooking. This will induce a sense of satiation and fulfillment.

34. Low Salt, Less Butter

Salt is infamous for causing bloating, whereas butter is famous for its high calorie content. You should avoid these two things, or use them in moderation. Try flavoring your food items, such as soups, pastas, meats, stews, etc., with stuff like onions, peppers, garlic, chili, etc. These kinds of flavorings are not only tasty, but they make food very healthy as well.

35. Go Meatless Once a Week

Although meat is very popular among people, it is also supposed to be quite unhealthy and hard to digest. It is especially not recommended when you are trying to lose weight. You should ideally adopt a meatless day, such as Meatless Monday, where you should ideally avoid meat and eat things like black beans, sweet potatoes, etc. These things are definitely healthier than meat but may not be as tasty. However, health is more important than taste, and so, you should definitely focus on health instead of taste.

36. Cut It Out

Food is not the only thing of concern when you are trying to lose weight. It is all about fooling yourself and your brain. You can do this quite effectively if you follow most of the tips given in this book. You can try and cut veggies and fruits into large chunks instead of cutting them into small pieces. Ideally, you should eat the fruit in whole form. When you have to chew a lot while eating, you get a false sense of satiation early, which can help you to reduce your food and calorie intake.

37. Think and Eat

Before taking a second serving, drink a glass of water, and then wait for a few minutes. If you still feel hungry, get that second helping; else, stop eating, and declare that you are finished.

38. Drink Your Coffee Black

If you love your regular coffee but want to lose weight, it's time to switch over to black coffee. You might think that having your regular coffee won't make much of a difference, but this kind of small switch will help in the long run. For a real coffee lover, there is no suitable replacement. So, if you can't switch over to herbal teas, at least try to take your coffee black.

Black coffee is pretty much a calorie-free beverage. When you compare the calorie count of a regular cup of black coffee or espresso to one with milk, sugar, chocolate, and other condiments, you will realize the difference it makes. One cup of espresso will only have a calorie or two in it. Sugar-laden coffee with milk can have nearly 600 calories in a single serving. All the extra flavorings and sweeteners you ask your barista to add will only pile up the calories in your diet. This means that your diet can only include coffee if you drink it completely black.

The chlorogenic acid in black coffee is said to help in speeding up weight loss. This element can help to slow down glucose production in the body, and thus, the production of fat cells is also reduced. In fact, you can also change the normal milk in your coffee to nut milk as a healthier alternative. Increasing brown fat activity can help in controlling blood sugar and blood lipid levels. The increase in calories burned will help you lose weight.

Experts have found that drinking black coffee helps in losing weight because it stimulates brown fat, which burns calories to help generate body heat. Brown fat is different from the other fat that is in your body. It burns sugar and fat to produce body heat when it is cold.

Coffee beans contain various biologically active substances that can affect your metabolism. Other than caffeine, it has theobromine and theophylline as well. Black coffee also has antioxidants that will boost your weight loss process. The caffeine will be effective in increasing metabolic activity and boosting energy levels. Many people drink coffee as a stimulant before they exercise every day. Caffeine blocks adenosine and increases the release of dopamine and norepinephrine. this will help you feel awake and energized. The caffeine from your black coffee will also help to reduce untimely food cravings and help your body burn fat with more efficiency. So, you can now enjoy your coffee without worrying about your weight.

39. Eat Your Dinner Early

Eating your dinner earlier is another great tip to help you control your weight. The modern-day lifestyle is quite unhealthy in many ways. We eat untimely meals or just skip them altogether. Eating a late dinner is a common habit among people who tend to be overweight. Some studies show that eating all your regular meals earlier in the day can help in boosting weight loss and suppressing hunger pangs. So, you have to start considering the fact that it is not just about what you eat but also about when you eat. Instead of having dinner at 10 p.m. or right before bed, you should consider fixing dinner time to around 7 p.m.

Trust us when we say that it can make a lot of difference. The last meal of your day should be early and light, and there are many reasons for it. Scheduling your meal timings helps in conditioning your internal rhythm. This rhythm of your body helps it adjust to changes in sleep, eating, digestion, etc. Your meal timings will thus have an effect on the regulation of your body weight, metabolism, and various other health factors.

When you eat your dinner earlier, it increases the duration of your overnight fast. The time between dinner and breakfast allows your body to burn extra fat. Fasting initiates a process called ketosis that helps the body burn stored fat. This means that you will be losing weight while you sleep if you just eat early. Early dinners are much better for your digestive system, and having healthy digestion will aid in weight loss. The later you eat your dinner, the more likely it is that the food will just lie in your intestines or get stored as fat instead of being used.

Eating late also increases the risk of indigestion and heartburn. This will indirectly affect the quality of your sleep. Avoid eating any midnight snack if you want a healthy circadian rhythm or are trying to lose weight. Eating at least a few hours before sleeping will allow the food to be digested, and you can sleep better in a sated state. A late dinner can also cause bloating and water retention in the body. However, you also have to maintain a healthy time gap between dinner and bedtime.

If you eat early but sleep too late, it will just cause other problems and make it easier for you to reach for unhealthy snacks. Start your day early with breakfast, and fix a meal schedule for the whole day. Go to bed within two to three hours of dinner. This will let your body adjust in a healthy way. Thus, you won't have to skip meals and starve yourself to lose weight. Just eat better food and earlier.

40. Be Patient

While you embark on this weight loss journey, patience is of utmost importance. You cannot and should not try to lose a lot of weight in a short amount of time. This is not going to help your body and will instead cause more harm. When you follow fad diets or starve yourself to lose weight, it is more likely that you will soon be gaining it all back again. You may even see the numbers on the scale go down if you don't eat for a couple of days, but that is not real weight loss. Most people embark on their weight loss journey to try and see amazing results in as little time as possible. A lot of people lack patience and give up on healthy eating or exercise when they don't see quick results.

When you are on a diet and establishing a new eating pattern for yourself, it is natural to experience some ups and downs. You will need to be patient while you are experiencing these highs and lows. There might be days when you go off the diet plan and eat things that are not really healthy for you. You need to be patient with yourself and not feel guilty about being unable to be as disciplined as you aim to be. You can always go back on a diet the next day. However, if you are impatient and let small slip-ups demotivate you, it will be harder to get back on track. You have to be forgiving and patient with yourself if you want to establish a healthy pattern and achieve long-term weight loss.

All the diet tips given in this book will work effectively and surely. However, there is no guarantee that they will give you the instantly gratifying results that you may be looking for. You won't lose 10 pounds in five days or fit into your skinny jeans in two weeks. The process will take time but will effectively help you lose and manage your weight if you remain persistent and patient. Being impatient will just cause you to get off track and have to start all over again.

Instead, you can utilize the dietary tips given here and allow yourself to make a healthy lifestyle change for better long-term results. You have to be patient and aim for sustained weight loss. Don't start binging on junk food just because the numbers on your scale don't show significant change in a month. Weight loss is not just about the numbers and quick changes in body shape. The healthy dietary changes will slowly but surely facilitate long-term weight loss and help you get fit and healthy again.

Chapter 3 – 20 Exercise Tips to Lose Weight

Dieting is just one part of the game or one side of the coin in weight loss. If you genuinely want to lose weight, mere dieting won't suffice and is not recommended at all. Instead, you should ideally add a regular workout plan to your routine.

Pairing good diet habits with regular workouts will help you lose weight more effectively. Some people find different excuses to avoid working out, but this activity is essential if you want to lose weight. You do not need to do any specific kind of workout; any kind of exercise is okay if you it helps you lose weight.

1. Commit to a Set Amount of Time

While many people commit to working out as their new year's resolution, few follow through. This is because of the lack of commitment and discipline. They don't really put in much thought or effort into when they're actually going to work out. If you want to lose weight, you have to be ready to commit to a set day and time for exercise. You also have to consider how long you will work out. It could be anything from 20 minutes to an hour; it is up to you. However, you have to stick to this timing and not stop before the timer runs out. If you have dedicated yourself to a 30-minute workout, stick to it. It may seem a little hard in the beginning, but if you push yourself, it gets easier. Soon, you will easily be able to increase the duration of your workout well beyond what you had initially planned on. Committing to your days and durations for workouts will actively help you lose a lot of weight. Diet and exercise will go hand in hand when it comes to weight loss. You cannot skip your workouts and expect the results you want to see.

2. Build a Workout Routine

Building a workout routine is important for weight loss as well. First, only doing cardio will not help you much. Cardio should definitely be a part of your workout but not the only exercise you do. When you are aiming for weight loss, you have to think about what kind of workout you should be doing. Planning a workout routine before you start will help you see better results and guide you along the way. Don't go overboard with cardio, and make sure you include at least some weight training. Weight training helps boost metabolism for a longer period than cardio does. So, mix the two, and create a routine for yourself. You can have three days of cardio with two days of strength training every week to start with. The days and duration of your workout will depend on you and your needs. Remember not to overdo it, and allow yourself recovery days. Similarly, you can switch up between different types of exercise on different days of the week according to your preference. Instead of going to the gym every day, you can even add a day or two or some sport that you like, such as tennis or swimming. Otherwise, fix your workout routine according to the different areas of the body that you want to focus on. On Mondays and Wednesdays, you can focus on the abs, while Tuesdays and Thursdays could be leg days. You get the drift. Just build on your personal workout routine. You can keep changing it along the way to see what works best. This will help you lose weight in the best way possible and see real results from your exercise.

Use these tips to build your workout routine:

- First, determine your situation. Are you just trying to lose weight, or do you want to build muscle and bulk up? Write down what your goals are so that you have a clear idea of what you want to accomplish from the workout. Then, think about how much time you can devote to working out. Dedicating 45 minutes to one hour a day would be ideal, but it isn't always possible for everyone.

However, you have to take some time to figure out what your possible workout duration is. You can develop the most efficient workout routine according to your workout duration. What you can accomplish in one hour can also be done in 30 minutes if you exercise the right way. Strength training can burn twice the calories that cardio does within half the time. You also need to figure out where you are planning to work out. It could be at home, at the gym, or even at a park. The place where you work out will help you determine the kind of training you can do. This is because you don't have the same equipment that a gym has if you exercise at home. Your workout has to be adjusted according to the tools you have at hand.

- The next step is to figure out what kind of exercises you should be doing. The best workout will be the one that you know you can actually stick with. Don't choose something that seems too difficult for you because it will set you up for failure. You don't need to make your workout routine too complicated. It should just be efficient and simple while helping you improve your body. To begin with, you should figure out a full body routine and do this at least three times a week. Ideally, you should try working out five days the week. Your routine should include exercises that work on every part of your body. There are specific moves designed for the quads and others for the butt and hamstrings. Quad exercises include squats, box jumps, and lunges. The hamstrings and butt will improve with deadlifts, step-ups, and hip raises. You will also need to do exercises for the push muscles that include your shoulders, chest, and triceps. These include bench press, push-ups, dips, and overhead press. Exercises for the pull muscles will focus on the back, grip, and biceps. This will include bent-over rows, pull-ups, and chin-ups. Dedicate some exercise for your core, which includes the abdomen and lower back. These exercises will include planks, mountain climbers, side planks, jumping knee tucks, and hanging leg raise. You can ask an instructor or just watch videos online to learn how to do all these exercises in the correct way. You can choose one exercise for each target area, and that will make up your workout routine for the week. You can switch up the exercises every other week to keep it fun. Focus on these basic exercises first, and get stronger. Then, you can move on to more complicated exercises to help you burn more calories. If you do compound movements that work on multiple muscles at once, you will only have to do a few exercises in your routine. Compound movements will make your workouts more efficient.

- You have to figure out how many sets and reps you should do. A set involves repetitions of an exercise without stopping. So, doing 10 crunches will mean one set of ten reps. Typically, you should first do a warm-up and then move on to the sets and reps. Try doing three to five sets for each exercise in a single workout. The reps per set can be seven to eight when you are first beginning. If you want to burn fat and build muscle at the same time, you should try at least 10 to 15 repetitions per set. If 15 reps are easy for you, increase the difficulty of that movement or increase the weights. When you do 1 to 5 reps, it helps in building strength and dense muscle. If you do 6 to 12 reps, you will be building muscle strength and muscle size. Doing more than 12 reps will allow you to build muscle endurance. Don’t stress too much about how many sets and reps you should do. To begin with, try lighter weights and more reps, and you can build from there. Just focus on getting stronger with each workout you do. These workouts should push you and help you burn as many calories as possible. If you don't strain yourself a little, you won't lose weight, even if you exercise for an hour.

- You need to keep track of how long you should wait between each set. The time can be adjusted according to how healthy the individual is. You need a small break between each set to rest, but the break should not be too long, just as much as necessary. If you are doing heavy lifting reps within the 1 to 3 range, rest for about 3 to 5 minutes. If you are doing 4 to 7 reps of strength lifting, rest for 2 to 3 minutes between each set. If you are doing 8 to 12 reps for size or strength, rest for a minute or two. If you are doing more than 13 reps to build endurance, just rest long enough to help you recover before the next set. You should just focus on doing the best that you can. So, your rest period between sets does not have to be a specific time that everyone else follows. It should just be enough to allow you to recover and repeat.

- You have to find the right weight that you should be lifting. Don't shy away from weights, even if you don't want to build a muscular body. Weights will help build strength, tone, and muscle. The more muscle you build, the more fat you will burn. Trial and error will allow you to determine how much weight you should lift. You have to lift enough to be able to get through your whole set, but not so much that you cannot do any more exercises after the set. It has to be between too heavy and too light. You can work with your body weight, but then you have to make your exercises a little more difficult over time. When 20 push-ups become easy for you, increase it to 25 to 30, and so on.

- How long should your workout be? Generally, 45 minutes of a workout routine is efficient in helping anyone burn their excess weight. If you do around 3 to 5 sets of 5 different exercises, you will find 45 minutes more than enough. However, you also have to figure in some time for warming up before the workout and stretching after you are done. If you increase the intensity of your workout, you can decrease the duration of it. A highly intense workout in lesser time will give you better results than if you did the opposite.

- How many days in a week should you train? Some people might tell you to exercise every single day of the week. However, we will tell you differently. Firstly, you may not have the time to do this. Secondly, you probably don't want to. You have to build a workout routine that you can continue for a long time. You cannot be training seven days a week unless you are a professional athlete. So, try at least three to five workouts every week. You get time to rest and pick yourself back up again if you follow this routine. Just try exercising every alternate day if you can't do it continuously. Otherwise, work out on weekdays and enjoy the weekend to rest. Just remember to exercise and stay active if you are serious about losing weight.

- Lastly, keep track of everything. Write down details about when you work out, what exercises you did, and how your weight is changing. It will help you maintain and adjust your workout in the long term.

Here is an example of a workout routine if you want to lose weight:

- Cardio twice a week. Each session should be at least 40 to 50 minutes.
- Strength training twice a week. Each session should be an hour.
- High-intensity interval training once a week. The session can be of 20 minutes.
- Keep two days of the week for active recovery.

It doesn't necessarily have to be this particular plan. It just has to be a routine similar to this that really helps you get active and burn the fat. Following a routine will help you strain your body in a healthy way consistently and thus lose weight. It's not a big deal if you miss a workout once in a while. However, you should definitely get back on track the next day.

3. Set a Schedule for Your Workouts

If you are serious about a regular workout, schedule a fixed time for it. Don't just try to fit your workout in here and there. This will only give you more opportunities to back out of it whenever you can grab the chance. When you make it a fixed part of your routine, it will grow into a lifelong healthy habit that you will thank yourself for in the long run. Make your workout a predictable task in your day. This will let you know that this particular time of the day is specifically assigned only for exercise. You cannot make excuses about being too busy the whole day to find time to exercise. So how do you commit time for a workout? Well, when you are just starting out, you have to try to work out at least 3 to 4 days a week. Fix those particular days in the week when you can make time to exercise. Next, figure out what time works best for you, and schedule your workout well in advance for those timings on those days. Plan it out well, and note it down on your phone calendar or just a note on the fridge. Don't budge from the plan.

4. Try High-intensity Interval Workouts

High-intensity interval training or HIIT is a workout that includes intense activity for a short period of time, followed by a low-intensity activity. HIIT is very convenient for people who usually have busy schedules. HIIT workouts can be as short as 4 to 7 minutes and are very versatile. Studies show that HIIT workouts tend to burn more calories and fat even if done only for a short period of time. The workout can also cause your body to be in hyper drive, because of which you burn calories as much as 24 hours after your workout. You can incorporate HIIT into your workout regimen. For example, you can run as fast as you can for 40 seconds, then rest for 20 seconds. You can also do bodyweight exercises for a determined amount of time and then rest afterwards. Moreover, there is a Tabata training method through which you can complete a workout in just 4 minutes.

5. Power Up Your Run

Running is probably the best cardio exercise there is. It helps in improving cardiovascular health and boosts blood circulation. Running can build the foundation for any other fitness activity. It's not just for losing weight. When you add strength training to your running, it is the best combination to lose weight and improve overall health. This is why you should consider powering up your runs. Don't just run continuously for 45 minutes on the treadmill. Instead, add exercises like squats and lunges in between the run itself. It will push your body to the next level and boost the fat burning process in a major way. You can start your warm-up and then do around 15 minutes of a moderately paced run. Then, add some burpees, lunges, squats, push-ups, or pull-ups in between. You can do all of these exercises between two running periods. You can also keep running and stop every couple of minutes from doing at least 30 seconds of any of these exercises. You need to endure at least 30 minutes of this kind of workout if you want to really boost your metabolism and burn more fat. Take time to cool down after this kind of workout. Run at a slower pace as you finish your power workout.

6. Switch It Up

Your body can quickly adapt to your fitness plan, so it is a good idea to switch up your cardio and strength training every now and then. The change doesn't have to be dramatic. You can increase the intensity or the duration of your workout. You can also try other fitness activities. Discovering a new sport or training method can be both fun and exciting. Try dancing classes, yoga, Pilates, Zumba, CrossFit, or any sport. If you are lifting weights, you should also gradually increase the weights to continue reaping benefits from the exercise. The main idea is to keep challenging your body to avoid a weight loss plateau.

7. Use High-quality Clothes While Working Out

It is important to wear the right workout clothes to keep you safe and comfortable throughout your workout. Wearing proper running shoes while jogging can prevent injuries and can also help you maintain your balance. It is difficult to stay focused on your workout if you are not comfortable. Choose clothes that are right for your body and offer flexibility so that you can move freely. Choose fabrics that have moisture-wicking properties. These types of fabric keep your skin dry and your body cool while you exercise. Women should also invest in a sports bra that provides adequate support.

8. Find a Workout Partner

Having a partner or buddy can motivate you to work out even when you are feeling lazy. Knowing that there is someone waiting for you can enable you to push your excuses aside and meet your fitness goals. Make sure that you find someone who can inspire you to do better.

Your spouse can be great workout partner as well. They are competitive but not crazy about it. You can even make this a romantic activity.

9. Choose Your Tunes

Workouts can be boring without music. Search for music that can get you in the mood to work out. There are several athletes who opt to listen to relaxing music while doing hard workouts, whereas there are those who opt for upbeat music. Choose music that can motivate you to do better in your workout. As a cautionary note, make sure that you are not playing your music too loud, especially when you are working out outdoors, so you can still hear cars and warning sounds.

There are many CDs and albums available in the market solely made for the purpose of exercise. You can find some soulful and classic Indian music for Yoga and some peppy music for aerobics in one CD. Check out the market, or browse online stores.

10. Pay Attention to Your Form

Make sure that you maintain proper form throughout your workout. Getting injured because of improper form while working out can only prevent you from achieving your weight loss goal. Enlisting the help of a fitness trainer for the first month can help you achieve proper form. You should also remember that you should never sacrifice your form to complete more repetitions or to lift heavier weights.

Exercise-related injuries are extremely common and painful as well. These injuries can be simple things, such as pulling a muscle, but can also be something horrifying like muscle or ligament tear, fracture, etc.

11. Do Compound Exercises

You can maximize your workout time by doing compound movements instead of isolated exercise. Isolated exercises like bicep curls can only work a particular muscle, whereas compound exercises can target multiple muscle groups at once. This means that you will get the benefit of a full-body exercise with just a few exercises. Compound movements are also beneficial for strengthening your body. Examples of compound exercises include lunges, squats, pull-ups, shoulder press, and bench press.

Some compound forms of exercises include dancing, dance aerobics, etc. These forms are highly effective and useful in losing weight in a very healthy manner.

12. Use the Body that You Have

Exercising in a gym that has various machines and equipment has its own advantages, but do not think that you cannot have a great workout without fancy equipment. There are many people who manage to exercise and lose weight through bodyweight training. Bodyweight exercises are movements that use your own body as a form of weight and resistance. These exercises include push-ups, burpees, and air squats. Bodyweight exercise is also recommended for people who don't have the time or budget to go to a gym.

It is a well-known myth that you need to be rich to gain weight and to lose it as well. It is also believed that you need to eat a lot of fancy stuff to lose weight and to gain muscles. If this were the case, then prisoners living in prisons would not look so buff and muscular. Instead, they would look weak, frail, and skinny. This sole fact debunks this popular myth.

13. Accept Discomfort

If you are overweight and unused to any exercise, you have to expect some discomfort. Don't assume that it will be easy. If you truly want to get fit, accept the initial discomfort as part of the package. Discomfort is not the same as pain. If you are in real pain or hurt yourself, you need to stop immediately, and seek medical attention. However, if you just stop your workout because you feel tired, it is not the same. This is why we emphasize the importance of fixing the duration for your workout as well. You cannot do 10 minutes of a run and give up. It will be tiring and tough initially, but you will get past that stage soon. You need to commit yourself to at least a month of a fixed workout routine. This whole month might seem long and tiring for you, but it will soon become a habit. You might experience some cramps and soreness when you exercise for the first week or so, but it is to be expected. You are pushing your body out of its usual comfort zone and changing your unhealthy routine to a better one. You have to know the difference between good "pain" and bad pain. If the first signs of discomfort make you stop exercising, you will barely ever exercise at all. The more effort you start putting into your workout, and the more you push yourself to a new level, the more discomfort you will initially feel. However, this passes, and you will soon be able to go through entire workouts without a break. The real pain is when you are injured or hurt yourself in some way while exercising. This is the only time you can excuse yourself out of a workout without guilt. Otherwise, learn to accept the discomfort, and look forward to the results and the achievement of your weight loss goals.

It is important that you know you will be sore from increasing activity, but it's crucial you know the difference between discomfort and pain.

14. Try Something New

So, exercise is obviously a crucial part of losing weight. However, exercise does not only mean going to the gym and doing strenuous workouts. There are many other ways in which you can exercise your body and even have fun while doing it. Why don't you try something new? This will motivate you and make you look forward to this form of exercise. Does the idea of rock climbing excite you? Well, this is also a form of exercise and would be a great way to lose weight.

Sign up for some rock climbing classes or sessions. If you like running, then don't just stick to the treadmill. Go out for a run around the park or new neighborhoods. This can be a refreshing change. Even better, you can sign up for a marathon. It will give you a goal to look forward to. Train for your marathon until the day comes, and you will reap the satisfaction of completing it.

Meanwhile, you will also be losing a lot of weight. Trying something new will motivate you to stick to your exercise schedule, even if you are bored with your usual workouts. You can even try some Pilates or Zumba sessions to switch things up. Working out does not have to be as boring as you expect it to be. A lot of these activities won't even feel like exercise, but you will be enjoying while reaping the benefits of burning a lot of calories.

The following are some great new ways to exercise while having fun:

- Hiking: Just put your hiking shoes on, and get out of your house. Explore different hiking trails near you. Get a hiking buddy, or join a group. There are many great hiking spots that you can explore, and you will be burning fat the whole time that you go on this adventure. Hiking is a great weekend workout activity to look forward to.

- Rock climbing: Rock climbing is a little more intense than some other activities. You have to be fit and be careful while you do it. This form of exercise is great for the arm, back, and forearms in particular. You can check what your level is, and go on the climbing route that is suitable for you. You can also go to a nearby center that teaches you rock climbing in artificial setups.

- Dancing: Dancing is one of the most fun ways to burn fat. Sign up for dancing classes, or just blast some music and dance by yourself. Swing dancing and hip-hop will get you drenched in sweat in no time. You can try Zumba or the Tango as well. There are so many different types of dancing classes you can sign up for; just choose something that catches your fancy. You will be learning something new, meeting new people, and losing a lot of weight along the way. Dancing will make you feel good mentally and physically.

- Martial arts: If you are an avid movie buff, you have probably been interested in martial arts at some point or the other. Use this opportunity to sign up and learn it now. You will burn calories and also learn self-defense. It will also make you feel like a real badass.
- Clean: Yes, cleaning is also a form of exercise. Nobody likes cleaning up their house or room, but it really gets you moving. So, play some music, and clean every inch of your room. It'll keep you active and also help you get something done. There's nothing better than coming home to a clean house. While you clean your house, you are also keeping your body fit.
- Yoga: Yoga helps in increasing flexibility and building strength, and it also helps you relax on another level. There are so many types of yoga you can try out, and it really works. While you will be burning fat, you will also improve your mental wellbeing.

Just try out any new activity that will get you up and about.

15. Don't Forget to Rest

Your desire to lose weight might just be too much that it pushes you over your limit. Make sure that you give your body enough time to recover. Do not work the same set of muscle groups in consecutive days. While it is important to challenge your body, it is also crucial that you do not push yourself to the point of fatigue and exhaustion. This can have a detrimental effect on your body and morale.

Sleeping is a very effective form of rest, but it can be a nuisance if you lead a busy life. Instead, try doing various breathing exercises and meditations that will help you to relax yourself and will help you to keep yourself active and well rested. Power naps should be incorporated in your day-to-day life as well.

16. Realize that You Can't Do it Alone

It pays to invest in a trainer if you are new to working out. A trainer can correct your form and observe your progress. Make sure that you find a trainer who has your best interest in mind. You can inquire about the trainer's experience and speak with his or her regular clients to understand his or her methods.

You can also ask for the help of like-minded people. There are a lot of people who are passionate about fitness and living a healthy lifestyle. You can join support groups that can provide you with more information on how you can achieve your own weight loss goals. Hiring a gym teacher is a great option as well, but it is costly. Ideally, a good friend who is fit or wants to get in better shape will be your best option. This kind of friend will keep you motivated, and the competition that arises from this kind of friendship will be a great motivator as well.

17. New Rewards

Have you reached any of your goals? If so, you should allow yourself to feel proud and pleased with yourself. You should also reward yourself. Build the habit of rewarding yourself each time you reach a new goal. This will go a long way in keeping you focused and motivated to keep improving.

Instead of indulging on fast food, snacks, or ice cream, treat yourself to some new gym gear. There are many really stylish brands you can choose from when you are looking at workout clothing. Spend some cash on a new outfit or gym shoes, and avoid the guilt that some rewards can cause. Maybe you have always wanted to start a home gym. Look into some equipment for your home. Buy a set of dumb bells, and use them at home.

Whatever you decide, the main thing is to change your attitude toward how you reward yourself. Rewards do not have to be unhealthy or bad for you. Change your attitude, as well as your body, so think healthy and stay healthy.

18. Track Your Body

Another rewarding way to keep track of your weight loss journey is to track the changes in your body and use pictures. A picture is said to be worth a thousand words, and this definitely holds true. When you're on a weight loss journey, seeing the changes with your own eyes will be much better than anyone else pushing you on. This will motivate you, even more, to keep going. When you see real results from all your effort, you will be more likely to keep going. You might not see drastic changes in a short period of time, but they will definitely happen slowly.

Most people are motivated to start on their weight loss journey in the first place because they want to improve their body image. They either want to look a certain way or fit into certain clothes. So, tracking the changes will not only motivate you but also help you notice if you are slacking. If you don't see any real changes, you will also know that you are doing something wrong. It will give you a chance to assess your workout routine and your diet as well. Nonetheless, the main purpose of tracking progress is to motivate you.

Take measurements of your body, and note them down in a diary according to date. However, don't keep taking measurements too frequently. It is impractical to expect to go from a size 10 to a size 8 in 5 days. Instead, measure yourself every 2 to 3 weeks. This will be a much more realistic method and also be more likely to show you changes.

Also, take pictures. Taking before and after pictures during a weight loss journey can be immensely motivating and gratifying. Take one picture of the same clothes and in the same poses once a week. Over the next few months, you can compare these pictures side by side and notice the difference. Don't aim for quick perfection, and instead, look forward to healthy improvement over time. Don't set a goal like becoming a size zero in 2 months. You can be a bigger size and still be healthy and fit. Use the measurement tracking and pictures to help you keep going on your efforts for weight loss. Even the slightest changes can be very important for your mental strength. Studies have shown that people who tried this particular tip were more likely to keep eating right and exercising than those who didn't.

Another study conducted at Columbia University showed that people who were trying to lose weight while being motivated by body image were more likely to succeed while they used this kind of tracking. So, it is not just about checking the number on your weighing scale because numbers can be deceiving. When you see pictures of yourself and how your clothes fit differently, you can definitely feel the changes in body weight yourself. Your pictures will always be a great reminder for you to see how far you have come with persistence, effort, and patience.

19. Watch Your Clothes

Clothes play a very important role in a weight loss regimen. As said earlier, try to use clothes that are highly comfortable and can absorb sweat.

You should also prevent and avoid baggy clothes and instead wear form-fitting clothes. Form-fitting clothes always remind you that you are supposed to be losing weight, and they do not let you forget about your regimen. Baggy clothes hide your body and, more often than not, this can lead to forgetfulness about your diet and exercise regimen. So, even when you are relaxing in your house, you should definitely wear form-fitting clothes that will keep you on track all the time.

20. Patience

Regular exercise is an important aspect of losing weight permanently. As we have mentioned earlier in the book, patience is of utmost importance in your weight loss journey. You have to exercise this patience even when it comes to working out. Be patient, and follow through with your workouts. Be patient as you wait for the results to show. Don't expect your workout to be very easy or for it to show you instant results. You are not going to lose 5 pounds in a couple of days, no matter how strenuous your workout regimen is. Your goal may be to build more muscle or to increase your flexibility. You could be aiming to lose overall weight or just in some areas. No matter what the goal is, you will have to be persistent and patient. You will reach your goal weight at some point, but you cannot be impatient about it. You will not see any changes happen overnight. However, if you establish a practical regimen of exercise that you are able to follow on a daily basis, you will be able to see results in the long term. It will be gradual, and you will have to put in day-to-day efforts. That is the only way you can see improvement. Patience and consistency are important. You may train extremely hard for weeks and then you may just give up one day. However, you have to keep exercising if you want your results to remain.

Don't stop exercising if you are unhappy with your initial results. Don't stop exercising if your waist measurement hasn't changed after 10 days. Don't stop exercising if you look the same as you did a month before you started working out. It takes different amounts of time for different people, and the results will vary as well. Don't get impatient if your workout buddy loses more weight than you did even if you started out together. Their body is completely different from yours, and you should just use this as motivation to keep going and aim for similar results. Do not expect instant results if you want long-term benefits from your exercise and dietary changes. Be patient, and see how your efforts pay off.

Chapter 4 – 20 Lifestyle Tips for Weight Loss

Deciding to lose weight can affect your entire life. There are countless fad diets and programs that promise quick fixes but do not offer real results. In fact, if you try to lose weight by doing fad diets, you can actually ruin your body and can cause many problems to your health. Moreover, the weight lost due to fad diets is not permanent, but the health problems arising due to these diets definitely are.

You cannot simply lose weight by dieting or just exercising. You need a lot of planning and also need to understand your body. To lose weight successfully, you should evaluate your lifestyle and change your negative and unhealthy habits. You need to drop those unhealthy foods and replace them with healthy albeit tasty stuff. You also need to work hard to drop those extra calories.

1. Change Your Mindset

Going through the process of losing weight can make you stronger and more confident. It will also help you realize some aspects of yourself. You will learn the kind of physical activities you enjoy and what healthy foods you like. Most importantly, you would understand the importance of maintaining a healthy weight. Your reasons for losing weight should go beyond wanting to "look good." You should also expect to feel better, more energized, and healthier after losing weight.

Remember, losing weight is not a physical thing; it is a state of mind. You cannot lose weight simply by concentrating only on the physical aspect. Similarly, weight loss not only affects your body but concerns your mind as well. You feel active, fresh, and happy.

2. Make It a Commitment, and Write It Down

Permanent weight loss takes time and effort. Once you decide to start eating right and working out, you should make it a life-long commitment. You should be ready to make permanent changes in your lifestyle. Write your goals down in your journal. Whenever you feel like you are losing motivation, read what you have written to remind yourself of your commitment.

Remember, commitment is the most important thing. As long as you are committed to your goal, you will stay put and concentrate on losing weight. As said earlier, read your journal to keep yourself on track. You can also try downloading an app to keep yourself committed.

3. Document Your Weight Loss

Documenting your weight loss can keep you motivated. You can keep a journal to record your thoughts. You can also take photographs of yourself before and after weight loss to help keep yourself motivated to continue with achieving your goal. Seeing how far you have come would also give you a sense of accomplishment.

Documenting your weight loss is not only a fun way to keep you motivated, but it is also a way to keep your habits and routine in check. Looking at your progress every day, even if it is just a little progress, will keep you motivated. You can achieve better results if you keep an eye on your progress. With this, you should ideally write everything down, including your measurements, your weight loss, your weight gain, your muscle gain, your BMI, calories, etc.

4. Morning Routine

If you want to lose weight, you need to start your day the right way. Your morning routine sets the tone for the rest of your day. There are a few things that you can start doing each morning to stimulate weight loss in your body. Everyone knows that waking up early and being a morning person is a healthy lifestyle habit. Studies show that those people who wake up earlier in the morning tend to be happier, healthier, and more successful. So, the next time that anyone advises you to wake up at dawn, you should really consider it, but for now, let's focus on the benefits of waking up early if you want to lose weight.

The following are some habits that should be a part of your morning routine if you want your weight loss journey to be more successful:

- Wake up as early as you can, and give yourself some time before you need to head out to work. Don't wake up 5 minutes before you need to rush out. This will prevent you from carrying out a healthy morning routine for yourself. Sleep earlier at night so that you get adequate sleep and feel well-rested in the morning. If you don't sleep well, skip breakfast, and go through the whole day tired, you are less likely to be a fit person.

- Drink some warm water as soon as you wake up. Drinking a tall glass of water will kickstart your body in the morning. Squeeze some lemon juice into the water for an added boost. This trick is considered helpful in burning belly fat. You can also try having a spoon of apple cider vinegar with water for the same reason. Staying hydrated the whole day will help you lose more weight. People often mistake their thirst for water for hunger and eat more when they drink less water. Drinking a glass of water before a meal will also prevent you from overeating because it gives you the sensation of feeling full. Water is actually a natural appetite suppressant that will work to your benefit. It is also helpful in enhancing your metabolism, and you will burn more calories. Starting your day by drinking a tall glass of water and staying hydrated will allow your body to remove toxins and wastes easily.

- Give yourself time to have a proper high-protein breakfast. Having a healthy meal in the morning will keep you fueled all day. It is also an important factor in preventing unhealthy food cravings between your main meals. Many people skip breakfast because they don't have time or just because they think it'll help them lose weight. However, it does the exact opposite. People who eat a regular breakfast tend to be fitter than someone who skips breakfast. However, you also have to consider what you eat. Your breakfast should be high in protein if you are aiming for weight loss. This means that you should eat more eggs, Greek yogurt, tofu, etc. Protein will help to reduce the level of ghrelin in the body. Ghrelin is also called the hunger hormone. Avoid eating sugary foods, such as cereals or any junk food. These will only add calories and increase your weight. If you eat the right foods in the morning, it will give you more energy and also aid in burning fat.

- Drink a cup of herbal tea or black coffee. The antioxidants and the caffeine will be helpful in giving you an added boost. It will also help you focus more in the morning and stimulate you to go through a morning workout.

- Try working out in the morning hours instead of the evening. Mornings are the best time in the day to get a workout in. Research shows that people who exercise in the morning will tend to consume fewer calories throughout the day. A morning workout is more effective in burning fat and extra weight around the abdominal area as compared to working out at any other time of the day. Set aside time in the morning to exercise in any form you like. It could be a run, a HIIT workout, or just a swim. Any of it will stimulate weight loss, reduce appetite, and help you burn more calories.

- Try to get some exposure to sunlight in the morning. You could just sit outside with your coffee for a few minutes or workout under the sun. Certain studies say that getting adequate exposure to sunlight in the day also plays a role in weight loss and overall health. An added bonus is that you will be getting some important vitamin D as well.

- Weigh yourself in the mornings. This is the time of the day that you should note down your weight. Don't be scared of the weighing scale, and don't judge yourself on the basis of the numbers. It will just give you an idea of your body weight and help you measure progress. Seeing the numbers reduce in the morning will also motivate you to keep working toward weight loss. It will also help you make any appropriate adjustments to your diet or workout routine. If you have gained weight, you need to exercise a little more and have better control over what or how much you eat. If the numbers are reducing, you are probably doing it right. This is why regular weighing can be a good idea in the morning.

- Set intentions for the rest of your day. Plan out what you are going to do on that day. Don't go through your day without any direction. It will prevent you from being as productive as you could otherwise be. Practicing mindfulness in the morning is also considered helpful for your physical and mental wellbeing. It will relieve stress and boost your focus. It will also help you in losing weight because you will have better control over your emotions and thoughts. You will be less likely to binge on junk food or do any emotional eating. Just take five minutes to be mindful every morning, and see the difference it makes.

Start implementing any of the above in your morning routine, and begin your day the right way.

5. Predefined Hours

Set a schedule for yourself. This can be an extremely useful tool throughout your life. You can define the hours you spend on all your tasks throughout the day. Set aside time on the previous night or in the morning, and make a schedule for yourself. Note down what task you will be doing at any particular time of the day. Don't drift through the day without any direction. Everyone could use the help of a schedule. Make sure you assign a particular time for all your meals and workout during that day. Don't try to squeeze it in between work. Your health is much more important than work. You will also be able to be more productive and successful if you eat well and take care of your body. So, when the clock strikes at 1 p.m., make sure you are eating your lunch. If you have set your workout time for 9 a.m., don't allow yourself to do anything else at that time. Similarly, you can focus solely on work on your predefined hours for work. Moreover, set a bedtime for yourself, even if it may seem juvenile to you. As we have mentioned earlier in the book, your body has a circadian rhythm that plays an important role. Setting a bedtime for every day will help your body function better. It will also help you lose more weight in the long run because of this fixed routine. So, take out time to define hours for all your tasks. It will work in your favor.

6. Find Your Motivation

Everyone has their own reason to lose weight. Make a list of the reasons why you want to lose weight to remind yourself to pursue your goal. For added motivation, you can also find motivational quotes that you can relate to.

You can also get motivated by reading or listening to successful weight loss stories. You will realize that everyone faces challenges while losing weight. You might even pick up some tips from people who have already successfully lost weight and maintained a healthy weight. If you do not know any such person in real life, the internet can always help you. There are many forums and websites online, dedicated solely to weight loss techniques and methods. You can find lots of people who have completed their journey of weigh loss or currently on their road to lose weight. You can also share your own journey on such platforms and thus gain a lot of support and motivation.

A lot of people have different ways to keep them motivated. Some people love to dance while some people love to have a chat with a loved one. Some people also like to read motivational books, both fiction and nonfiction. Some people also like to sing or listen to music to motivate themselves. Choose your own way. If you have a hobby, such as gardening, etc., you should take it up and have fun doing it. This fun portion will refresh your mind and will make you more active and dedicated to achieving your goals.

7. Plan a SMART Goal

Simply wanting to lose weight is not enough. You should also set a SMART goal to achieve it. SMART stands for specific, measurable, achievable, relevant, and time-bound.

A specific goal is much easier to accomplish than a broad one. Keep it measurable by tracking your progress regularly. This way, you will know whether you are on the right track. Achievable goals mean that they are not too extreme. You shouldn't expect yourself to change overnight. Have the patience to achieve your goal gradually. Relevant goals mean that they are important to you. Remind yourself constantly of why you want to lose weight in the first place. Time-bound means that you have to set a reasonable deadline to achieve your goal. This establishes a sense of urgency and prevents your goal from being overtaken by your daily activities.

If you decide to start eating more vegetables, then you should determine a way to start incorporating them into your diet. If you want to work out, then you should set a time and place to do it. It is also equally important to follow through with whatever strategy you decide on.

Do not set unrealistic goals and then try to achieve them. More often than not, these unrealistic goals are impossible to achieve and, thus, can actually break your confidence and dedication. It is a good thing to have a long-term goal, but you should also have small, short-term goals. These short-term goals will help you achieve the final goal quite easily.

8. Sharing is Caring

Your colleagues and friends can help you a lot in your weight loss endeavors. You should inform your colleagues about your weight loss goals and progress so that they can keep an eye on you. You can also invite them for a post-work dance class or some healthy activity. This will not only help you to lose weight but you also form a close bond with your colleagues and make your work place a happy place.

9. Get a Sipper

One of the main culprits of ruining your diet and exercise routine is craving. You have read a lot of ways to curb these cravings till now. You can also adopt a very easy way to curb the cravings in an office. You should buy a sipper and fill it with water or green tea or some other healthy and calorie-free or low-calorie drink. Whenever you feel hungry, drink from this sipper. Do not hesitate to refill it. The more you drink from this sipper, the less you will feel hungry. Staying hydrated will also keep you satiated, will curb your hunger, and will keep you active and alert as well. It will also prevent bloating, which is a side effect of consuming too much fiber without water. You can also use a simple reusable bottle if you do not have a sipper.

10. Change Your Eating Habits

It is not only eating that is important but also eating habits. There are some habits that you can adopt to enhance and help your diet routine. You should ideally sit in front of a person and eat with him or her instead of eating in front of a screen. This way, you will not eat randomly or mindlessly and instead eat properly. You should also concentrate when you are eating. You should brush your teeth after every meal so that you can avoid eating or snacking mindlessly.

11. Don't Follow Crazy Diets

A common mistake that a lot of people make when they embark on a weight loss journey is to follow a crazy diet. There seem to be a number of fad diets out there, and people fall prey to the false claims made by the promoters of these diets. However, numerous studies have shown that such fad diets can cause a lot of harm to the body and do not show long-term results, even if they help you lose weight initially.

It is actually quite easy to spot a fad diet. They promise quick results and promote some magical product or diet plan. They usually make you cut down on most of the nutritious food that your body really needs. They will probably tell you to completely cut off carbs or fats even though they are important food groups. There will be rigid rules to follow, and it will require a lot of effort on your part to follow through with such fad diets. After all, it isn't easy to drink only juice for an entire day or eat the same vegetables for the whole week. The point is, whenever you notice a diet like this, it is most likely unhealthy and ineffective.

All the weight loss tips mentioned in this book are to help you make conscious and healthy changes that will help you in the long run. It is not about following a liquid diet, fasting for days, skipping meals, or only eating soup for a month. These are the kind of crazy diets that most people try at some point or the other when they want to lose weight fast. Many times, you might see a drop in your weight after a week of following this type of diet, but it will definitely come back on sooner rather than later. Many such crazy diets will prevent you from providing your body with the nutrition that it really needs. Eating carrots or having cabbage soup for a week will not benefit your body in any way. You don't have to skip meals and stick to a single meal a day, either. In fact, this kind of diet plan sets you up for failure. You will soon be hungry and tired beyond measure. It will make you lean back on your old unhealthy habits and eat more to make up for the hunger. If you skip your timely meals, you will experience untimely cravings that will just cause more weight gain. You don't have to go on a juice cleanse to lose weight either. Homemade juices and smoothies are a great addition to your healthy diet. However, you cannot substitute all your meals with them. Your body knows how to cleanse and detoxify itself if you just eat the right kind of food. Switching to liquids for too long will have a negative effect on your digestive system as well. When you try switching back to your normal solid meals after a juice cleanses, your body will have difficulty in digesting the food.

Fad diets tend to cause the following symptoms:

- You will be dehydrated. You might be happy to drop pounds as fast as possible, but it won't be a long-term weight loss. Most of the weight loss from such diets is just water loss. You are dehydrating your body at this time, and the loss of the water weight is fooling your weighing scale. This kind of rapid dieting will only cause you to gain back the weight soon after, and you will have to follow a crazy diet again.

- You will experience nausea. The dehydration and fatigue from fad diets will make you feel nauseous. You may also get headaches. Your body is telling you that it is not getting the nutrition that it needs.

- Your digestive system will be affected, and you may suffer from constipation. It will also affect your metabolism.

Cutting off calories altogether will slow down your metabolism in a major way. You need a diet that prompts your metabolic system to work faster over time. You need adequate calories, carbs, protein, and fat to maintain the upkeep of your body.

- You will lose muscle. Don't follow a diet that just makes you eat less and doesn't guide you on exercise. If you diet without exercise, you will slowly be losing muscle from your body. When you lack adequate muscle tissue, your body will be unable to burn as many calories as it should. Muscle mass is important for the body and for you to lose weight. So, you have to exercise and build muscle while you follow a healthier diet.

- You will feel weak and fatigued. You will be hungry and thirsty when you follow a fad diet. You may be willing to go through this to lose weight fast, but it is a way for your body to tell you that you are doing something wrong. It will prevent you from being productive and doing any of your other tasks as well. If you starve yourself, you will be tired and won't feel like exercising. This will mean you are affecting your weight loss plan in the long run because the body needs to be active in order to burn calories.

Given that such diets are unhealthy, they will give you the same symptoms as those that you experience when you are ill. They prevent you from consuming the adequate vitamins and minerals that your body needs. So, be more aware of what any diet asks of you, and follow only one that is actually providing your body with the nutrition it needs. A balanced diet is crucial, even if you want to lose weight.

12. Walk and Talk

A lot of our daily communications and conversations now happen over the phone; some people even talk for hours altogether on phones. Instead of sitting at one place while talking on a phone, you should pick up your mobile phone and then walk around your house or a park while talking. If you talk daily for an hour on the phone, you will automatically walk for an hour, too; thus, you can have your cake and eat it, too. Caution should be taken while trying this thing though, as you should not walk and talk while you are on the streets or in a busy area because this can prove to be fatal.

We also use text messages or instant messaging services nowadays for most of our conversations. You can try doing the walk and talk thing for this as well, but unfortunately, this can lead to headaches. Instead, you should just cut the use of instant messaging; get up, leave your place, approach the person, and talk to him or her. This is obviously only possible if you are in the same building. This will not only help you to walk, but it will also make you more productive.

You should also set reminders on your phone or watch to go out for a short walk throughout the day. You need to follow these reminders very strictly though; else, they are of no use at all.

13. Do Not Focus Too Much on the Scale

Too many people are obsessed with the number on the scale. While it can be one way to measure your progress, be sure that you are also paying attention to how you feel. Once you focus on the other benefits of a healthy diet and exercise aside from weight loss, you'll remember how satisfying it is to do these things for yourself, and you can become even more motivated.

However, this does not mean that you should not have a look at the weighing scale once a week. Monitoring your weight once a week can really help you as this is one of the best ways to check your progress, and even if your progress is not huge, it will still help you to stick to your routine.

14. Make It Fun

Losing weight shouldn't feel like a chore. You can also have fun while doing it. For example, you can invite your friends to try healthy meals the next time you hang out. You can also turn exercise into a social experience, and do it with your family and friends. You can even add some friendly competition to your workouts. Engaging in fun activities increases your chances of doing these activities again.

Exercise can be made into a very activity quite easily. If you have always wanted to dance, try to pick up a dance form that is peppy, fast, and involves a lot of body movements. Hip hop, tango, tap dance, Kathak, polka, and street dancing are some common dance forms that double as good exercises. You can also pick up belly dancing if you want to tone your muscles as well. Nowadays, dance forms like Zumba, dance aerobics, musical aerobics, etc., are becoming quite popular, too.

To make dieting an interesting ordeal, you can try making a game out of your meals. Although this might seem odd, stupid, and, in a lot of cases, downright disrespectful, if you make meals more enjoyable, you can actually keep yourself on track and follow your diet routine very closely. Having competitions is a really good method to gulp down those unappetizing veggies and soups. Playing fun or soothing music while dining can also help. As said earlier, if you socialize while eating food, you can probably eat the most unappetizing meal ever without much of a problem.

15. Use Tools and Gadgets to Help You

You are blessed to have the advantage of modern technology. There are tools, gadgets, and applications that you can use to help you achieve your goals. You can use your smartphone to download running, exercise, and even healthy cooking apps. There are also gadgets, such as heart rate monitors and step counters, that can help you measure your progress. Nowadays, you can find wonderful apps for your smartphone. These apps can turn your phone into a pedometer, compass, etc. Some apps also choose the best workout music, which is very peppy, to keep you fresh and motivated for a long time. There are some innovative apps online that can actually enhance your overall exercise or walking experience with the help of virtual reality. Try to search apps online, and use them according to your needs.

16. Learn to Celebrate Each Accomplishment

There are times when the scale won't budge, no matter what you do. Instead of letting this discourage you, you should set other goals that do not include weight loss. For example, you can set a goal of completing a half-marathon or learning a new sport or dance. Celebrating each accomplishment can inspire you to stick to your program. When you achieve goals, you can reward yourself by buying something that you really want or pampering yourself for a day. Some people even treat themselves with a little portion of their favorite non-healthy food. Celebrating each little accomplishment is very helpful because it gives you something to look forward to. You will always some excitement and anticipation that will make you work harder and with more sincerity. However, always remember that if you are going to treat yourself with your favorite food, think about the portion. Do not eat too much; keep in mind that this is a treat and not a feast.

17. Put Your Excuses Away

People can find a hundred excuses not to lose weight. It might be because they don't have the time or find it too difficult. However, these excuses are primarily psychological. Common excuses include, "I do not have good exercise equipment," "I get tired when I do exercise," or "This exercise is not meant for me." All of these are just excuses, and nothing else. There are numerous ways by which a person can successfully lose weight without fancy equipment or expensive diet pills. It is said that man is the biggest critic of himself. Make sure that you suppress your inner critic, and find a way to overcome your excuses. You should learn to motivate yourself all the time, and avoid demoralizing yourself. Do not make any excuses because excuses are double-edged swords. Not only do they prevent you from doing your exercise routine or following your diet now, but they also have psychological effect that can ruin your future weight loss plans and routine.

18. Tackling Necessary Restaurant Visits

Sometimes, you simply cannot avoid going to a restaurant and eating out. These are mostly the social occasions that are unavoidable because of their importance, such as a boss's birthday, etc. However, this does not mean that you have to break your regime and forget about your diet. You can easily avoid the foods that can ruin your diet and actually continue with your diet even in the restaurant. You can do this in the following ways:

- If you are supposed to go to a fast-food joint and cannot avoid it at all costs, you should get a vegetable burger instead of a meat burger. More often than not, veggie burgers have less calories and are healthier than the meat ones.

- If you are supposed to go to a high-quality restaurant, then you should visit its website. Nowadays, a lot of restaurants upload their menus online with complete details of each of their dishes, including the calorie count, nutrients, etc. If you plan ahead and order your researched dishes when you go to the restaurant, you can avoid eating high-calorie products. Keeping these healthy options in mind can help you to keep high calories at bay while continuing with your diet effectively.

- If you are supposed to go to a restaurant that has no website or does not upload its menu, you should ask others about it. If you are not comfortable in doing so, you should only order things that are baked, boiled, grilled, broiled, steamed, blackened, etc., and never things that are fried or breaded. Even shallow fried things should be avoided.

- You should also eat something before going out to a restaurant. Eating something healthy, such as a handful of almonds, before going out to eat will actually help you to avoid overeating.

- Eat salad, and you can do so to start your every meal every time. It will help fill you up and help you eat less of the actual meal. This will help you cut the calories and thus keep you on track with your routine.

- More often than not, the proportion of calories in a dish increases because of condiments, sauces, etc., so when you go to a restaurant, you should ideally ask for all the sauces, condiments, dressings, etc., on the side so that you can add them according to your taste. These dressings can even make a simple salad very fatty, so remember this tip always.

- If you are supposed to go to a fast-food joint or even in a restaurant, order baked potatoes with skin instead of French fries. Eat the skin as well.

- Entrée is normally served on a bed of pasta, mashed potatoes, or something similar. Instead of this, you can ask the waiter to serve it on a bed of greens, onions or something similar. This is a very healthy alternative.

- If you love wine and simply cannot resist it when you are in a restaurant, order single glasses instead of a bottle.

- Do not worry; you do not have to skip your dessert. You can always enjoy dessert, but instead of eating a complete desert, try and share it or split it. You can also order a large desert and then share it with your whole party.

Losing weight and achieving your ideal body are only half the battle. Weight maintenance can be just as difficult as losing excess weight. There are many examples of people who have lost weight very quickly but gained it back even more quickly. This happens because people go back to their original gluttonous and unhealthy lifestyle as soon as they lose weight and achieve their target. Losing weight is not a process that ends; it is a lifelong, prolonged process. You need to follow some rules throughout your life if you want to stay fit, healthy, and active. These rules are not hard to follow, and anyone with a little motivation and determination can adhere to them quite easily.

Remember, the key to maintaining your ideal weight is to keep up the lifestyle, diet, and exercise habits that you have adopted while still trying to lose weight. You obviously do not need to follow the steps that seem too difficult when you were trying to lose weight, but you should definitely follow the steps that are highly important and essential to lose weight and keep it off.

19. Patience Matters

Even while you apply these lifestyle changes, patience will matter. It can be difficult at first, but following a healthy lifestyle is much easier than you might think. You will be a little reluctant and even uncomfortable with changing your eating, exercising, and living habits at first, but this is necessary. If you are truly motivated to lose the excess weight, get fit, and take control of your body again, you must put in the effort. Focus on combining healthy eating with a more active lifestyle. Don't laze around if you want to burn more fat. Make small changes that you can follow all your life to stay healthy. Be patient, and don't rush yourself with some drastic changes. Eat all your meals, but reduce the size of your portions. Stop eating once you feel sated. You don't have to keep on eating until you feel full. Don't berate yourself for being unable to skip meals because you shouldn't be doing that in the first place. Be patient, even while you are eating your food, and savor it. Eating too quickly and not chewing will make you eat more than you need. Wait for all the scheduled meal times before you eat again. Don't expect yourself to make all the changes at once. It takes a little time to be really consistent with such things. However, if you stick to a healthy morning routine, exercise regularly, eat a balanced diet on time, and rest well, you will soon see the results of your patience and persistence. Slow down, and don't rush things; you are aiming for long-term changes for an improved body and life.

20. Understand the Reason

It is easy to read about all the healthy habits and changes that you should be making in your life. You may even motivate yourself at first to follow through with all of it. However, you won't be able to do it for long if you don't understand the reason for all of these changes. There is a reasoning behind all of the changes that you are being asked to make. There is a reason for everything that you should do. You also have to find the real reason behind why you want to embark on this weight loss journey in the first place. Think of how being overweight and unfit affects your mind, body, and life in general. Consider all the benefits of making some small lifestyle and diet changes to counteract any of the negativity associated with excess weight. Your body will be much healthier, and your mind will be sharper and happier as well. When you understand the reason for everything, you are more likely to be motivated and persistent in all that you do.

Chapter 5 – 20 Tips to Maintain Weight Loss

Now that you know all the best tips to lose weight, let's talk about how you can maintain that weight loss. The weight loss journey does not end once you reach the goal weight you had aimed for. You may have lost the excess 20 pounds, but that does not mean that you can go back to your old habits. A lot of people gain back all their old weight when they fail to understand the importance of maintenance. You may be strict and persistent throughout your diet, but it is easy to fall back on old habits. You can start eating and living the way you used to when you were overweight again. This will just diminish all the progress you have made. This is why you need to learn some tips to help you keep off the excess weight and maintain a healthy body throughout your life.

1. Write Down Why Your Goals Matter

As you start on your weight loss journey and even as you continue on it, you need to remember why your end goals matter. You may have set certain goals for yourself and thus embarked on making a change in your life in terms of food, habits, and health. However, no matter how motivated you are in the beginning, it can be easy to lose sight of your goals. This is why you should try writing it down.

Make a small note to yourself about why these goals matter to you. What is the main reason that you want to make all these changes for yourself? Think of the difference it will make in your life when you manage to achieve these goals. Write them down one by one. Is it about how you look, how you feel about your health, or even about what people think of you? No reason is too big or too small. In the end, it has to be for you and how it helps you improve your life.

Once you note down the reasons for your goals, keep the list safely with you. It will be a constant reminder of why your goals matter. You may get off track during your weight loss journey or just feel demotivated. At this point, you can read your list again and remind yourself of the importance of your goals. Some people think that losing weight is just about looking better, but it is a lot more than that. Don't give up on your goal once you have set your mind on it. Remind yourself of all the reasons why you began in the first place.

2. Create Goals for the Week

Plan out your week in advance. Set aside time on your day off, and plan out the week ahead. This is important during the weight loss plan and after. It will help you stay on track and give you a sense of accomplishment when you follow through with your plan. Making a commitment is important. Don't assume that you will somehow find time during the week to get your exercise done. More often than not, you will skip your daily exercise.

If you don't have a fixed plan, you are less likely to do the things that you don't really want to do. Everyone struggles with this, so it is understandable. However, you have to take control and prevent a relapse to your old habits. Set aside time for a daily workout, and follow the plan every day. Set goals like the amount of weight you want to lose for the week or how many miles you want to run by the end of the week. If you need to lose some extra weight, set a goal for the week.

Check your weight at the end of the week to see if you met the goal by adjusting your weekly diet and activities. You can also set goals like deciding what kind of meals you will be having the whole week. If you tend to eat out quite often, take the initiative and try to avoid a single meal outside for the whole week. Eating home-cooked food is always a healthier alternative and will facilitate weight management. When you eat out, you cannot control all the ingredients or the method of cooking for your food. So, setting such small goals for yourself will be very helpful. You have to be focused if you want to stay committed to the goals of weight loss.

Changing your habits will require consistent physical and mental energy. So, make plans to address any other stresses in your life that aggravate your unhealthy habits as well. This will improve your ability to focus on managing your habits and weight. Your goals should be realistic and focused on the week. Dealing with one small thing at a time will be possible without too much stress. As you keep completing your weekly goals, you will find it easier to continue the weight management for a longer time. Think of the process, as well as the outcome, when you set your goals.

3. Chain Your Events and Goals

Link your weight loss goals and any other events together. When you create a schedule or plan for yourself, it will allow you to do so. No matter how busy you are, there can always be time. You just have to make the time. Your event schedule might be erratic and unpredictable at times, but you can still adjust your goals to accommodate them. It is not necessary to work out at the exact same time every single day. If you know that you will have some work at the time that you usually workout, then sneak a workout in when you are free that day.

It is understandable to skip a workout when you really have no option. However, if you skip from one day to another, you are just going back to your old ways. If you don't manage your time and goals in the appropriate way, you will be unable to achieve any of the goals you have set for yourself. If your goal is to eat healthier, don't eat junk food just because it is a business lunch. You can easily order something healthy off the menu. Most restaurants will accommodate any simple adjustments to their dishes as well. If you want to consume fewer carbohydrates, make the right switches.

When you eat a hamburger, ask them to give you the patty with some greens and without the buns. Instead of mayonnaise, you can ask for a lighter dressing. Such simple requests are usually accepted by restaurants if you don't make any unreasonable demands. This way, you are sticking to healthy eating even when you eat out. If your goal is to stick to a particular calorie count, use online apps to check how many calories a certain dish has when you eat out. It is actually much easier than you would expect it to be. So, plan it all out.

If you are the one hosting such lunches out, you can do your research and find a restaurant that has really healthy food for you, too. Similarly, make an effort to chain your new lifestyle in with your other commitments. Don't use excuses to back out of what you have decided to do for yourself.

4. Follow a Consistent Routine

Building your own fitness habit can take a long time. This habit becomes easier to sustain if you have a consistent pattern. For example, you can choose to work out in the morning before going to work. Waking up at a specific time each day can condition your body to adapt to the pattern and make it easier for you to form this habit. You can always mix up the activities, but try to maintain a consistent time pattern. Make sure you stick to this even if you do not feel motivated to work out for the day. Remember, constant vigilance is the best motto for everyone who is trying to lose weight.

5. Use a Plan that Works for You

There are a lot of diets in the world, but the best is the one that you can maintain for a long period of time. Everyone has his or her own preference. Do not force yourself into a lifestyle that does not feel natural. Look for a plan that you can maintain for the long term. If you cannot honestly see yourself giving up carbohydrates, then look for a diet that provides flexibility. With this, if you plan a diet according to your need and body, you can actually increase the rate of weight loss without causing any problem or harm to your body.

6. Follow Your Plan

If you make a plan, you need to follow it. Don't just create a schedule and then leave it lying around. Use it to guide you through your days and weeks. It may seem boring or monotonous, but you will be grateful for the results it will give you. Following your plan will mean that you are efficient in achieving the goal you have set for yourself. If you drift from your plan too much, you will be less likely to see the results that you are aiming for. Don't assume that you will be able to make it work somehow without following a plan. There is a reason that a plan is being made in the first place. It can be easy to drift from one thing to another.

Following a schedule will keep you on track, even though you will have to exercise some self-discipline. The point of the plan is that you take time to figure out how you can best utilize your time and energy to achieve a particular goal. Once you create this plan, you just have to follow it. However, when you drift away from the plan, you have to constantly worry about what you should or should not be doing. This will most definitely sabotage your ultimate goals. When you are trying to maintain a healthy weight, create a healthy routine for yourself. This way, you will not compromise the effort that you put in to lose all the excess weight over time. So, follow your plan and maintain your health to lead a better quality of life.

7. Stay Active

You will need to maintain your current fitness level to maintain your current weight. Studies show that just by simply walking extra 2,000 steps or for about 20 minutes each day, people can successfully avoid excessive weight gain. You should ensure that you are physically active most days of the week.

Regular exercise must be a part of your healthy lifestyle. You do not just stop once you have achieved your weight goals. Do exercises that you find enjoyable so that you are more likely to stick to them. It is said that a 30-minute brisk walk a day can keep you healthy without much trouble. You should definitely try this option if you do not have much time. Even then, if you cannot take out time for a 30-minute walk, then you can always divide it into 5-minute instances.

You can also adopt some simple exercises to keep yourself active throughout the day. These exercises should be easy enough that you should be able to do them even when you are sitting in a chair. Exercises, such as breathing exercises, simple yoga, walking around your office, etc., are easy to do and will keep you active without interrupting your daily schedule.

8. Don't Skip Days

You need to understand the importance of consistency. It would have been a hard change for you when you first started working out regularly in the first place. Maybe your weight goal motivated you at the time. This might have kept you going to the gym or just working out consistently. However, many people start skipping days when they have achieved their goal. You might not have to do a hardcore workout to lose weight like you previously did, but you still need regular exercise.

If you skip days and start getting lazy, your body will stop burning calories as well. You need to maintain the new habit that you have created. You get your rest days, and maybe you can add another rest day once you have achieved your goal. But you still need to keep exercising on the other days. The intensity of the workout can be adjusted according to your goal of losing more weight or just maintaining your present weight. Professional athletes, bodybuilders, etc. do not stop working out once they have finished a race or achieved that ripped body. They continue to stay active and persist in their effort because they know that they can easily lose what they have gained.

In the same way, you can easily gain back all the weight you lost if you start slacking. The worst part is, the time it would take to gain back the weight is much shorter than the time it took you to lose it. You can have rest days every week. However, fix days for working out, and follow through with them. One skipped day can easily become two and more. Pretty soon, you will find yourself going through the same old struggle to try and get back on track. It would just be simpler to follow through with your dedicated time for a workout every week. This will allow you to enjoy the benefits of the healthy body that you have attained for yourself. Skipping your workouts will make you feel unfit from fit, faster than you can imagine. So, stick to your days if you want to keep feeling good about your body.

9. Keep Stress at Bay

Stress can push you to make unhealthy choices. Even if you eat healthy and exercise, too much stress can make you gain weight. Stress can trigger adrenalin and cortisol, which cause your body to feel hungry even if you are not. When stressed, most people have cravings for sweets, as well as high-fat and salty foods, because these foods stimulate the brain to produce pleasure-inducing chemicals that can counteract the tension experienced by the body.

Moving your body is an effective stress reliever. It can aid your blood circulation while enabling cortisol to be flushed out of your body. You should also do activities that you find relaxing on a regular basis to prevent stress from accumulating.

Stress can also enhance the problems that are considered to be the side effects of obesity. Stress can lead to problems of the heart, brain, and nervous system. Sometimes, people are stressed about their extra weight, but as said above, stress can actually lead to weight gain; thus, this forms a vicious cycle. To break free of this cycle, you need to cope with stress effectively. Meditation and yoga are highly effective in controlling and countering stress. You should try breathing exercises and Pranayama as well. These few things will help you a lot to control stress.

10. Sleep Well

The body needs a proper amount of rest to function well. Proper amounts of sleep can also help replenish your energy and help your muscles recover from your workouts. Make sure that your bedroom is conducive for sleeping. Condition yourself to see your bedroom as a place for sleeping and relaxation. Moreover, it is better if you do not rely on stimulants to control your sleeping patterns because these chemicals can become addictive and may cause you to become dependent on them. It is highly advised to get at least six to seven hours of sleep every night. This sleep will keep you active, rested, and healthy.

11. Avoid Unplanned Eating and Drinking

Eating unplanned meals can cause you to overeat. Make sure that you schedule snacks throughout the day to manage your hunger. Planning your meals can also ensure that you are eating a well-balanced diet. This enables you to have all of the nutrients that you need to keep your body energized and healthy. You should also mix up your meals every week so that you don't get bored eating the same foods each day. A boring and repetitive diet can prove to be a great challenge and problem if you are trying to lose weight, so keep it fun.

12. Plan and Set Reminders

A planner or online calendar can keep you organized. You can schedule your workouts and treat them just like any other business appointment. You can also place reminders and motivations in a place where you can easily see them. Reading a few words of encouragement can spark your motivation. You can even create your own motivational board. Cut out pictures, quotes, or anything that can inspire you. Stick them on a wall or cork board. Nowadays, everyone has a smartphone, and there are many apps available online that can help you to track your routine and set reminders as well. Use these apps effectively, as they are free of any hassles and are extremely user-friendly and easy to use.

13. Make Sure You Have a Healthy Perspective on Food

Food is the main fuel for our bodies. Emotional eating can be described as using food to escape from your problems. Certain foods may trigger the release of feel-good hormones in the body but do not actually make everything okay. Be aware of the real reasons why you overeat or crave unhealthy foods. Avoid eating for the wrong reasons. Keep a log of the instances in which you ate for reasons other than hunger. You should also maintain the good eating habits that you have established when you were still losing weight. It is extremely important to understand that losing weight alone is not important; what is more important is maintaining the lost weight. Some people lose weight easily but struggle to maintain the lost weight. If you are one of these people, try hard to keep weight at bay.

14. Maintain a Positive Mindset

Negativity can only make you feel bad. Remember that a healthy lifestyle is about balance. Do not be depressed if you fail once in a while. This does not mean that all of your efforts are wasted. Just do your best to get back on track. Finding your own methods of maintaining weight can make you feel good about your accomplishments. Dwelling on positive thoughts can also motivate you. As said above, losing weight is not at all about physical strength and power; it is more about how mentally strong you are. If you keep your mind healthy and active, you will lose weight in no time.

15. Fuel Your Body Before and After Workouts

It is advisable to have a snack or workout shake before and after exercising. Choose a snack or shake that is rich in good carbohydrates and protein. Such foods can increase the flow of amino acid into your muscles and stimulate muscle growth and strength. It is particularly important that you nourish your body after workouts to prevent starvation and fatigue. Do not choose any fatty or unhealthy snack. These snacks are not only unhealthy for you, but they provide low to zero nutrition. Ask your dietician or check online for snacks that are healthy, full of nutrition, and can be consumed without any problems as such.

16. Be Inspired; Don't Compare

You are not the only person struggling with weight issues. A large percentage of people around the world have faced weight-related issues at some point in their life. The modern-day diet and lifestyle are some of the main causes of obesity in people of our generation. If you look up weight loss stories, you will find many inspirational people who have worked hard to turn their life around. You need to find inspiration from them, and keep going.

You may even notice your workout buddy or other people in the gym making progress. This can be quite intimidating for most people, especially when your personal progress is quite slow. However, remember that everybody is different. If someone else is losing weight and getting more fit, you should focus on finding inspiration from them. Don't envy them and demotivate yourself. Try to learn if they are doing something different that might help you as well. You can use them as your guide to improve yourself. A lot of these people will be very willing to help you out, too.

Don't compare your body and progress to someone else's. They are a completely different person, and weighing less does not make them better than you. When you start on a weight loss journey with someone else, it may seem natural to compare your progress with the other person's. This is especially true when you are both doing the exact same thing, but the other person is making better progress. However, you have to understand that there can be different reasons for this. His or her metabolism might just naturally be faster than yours. Do not let this be a reason for you to berate yourself and give up.

Comparison can actually do more harm than good. You don't need to try and become the same dress size as the other person. People lose and gain weight at different rates, and bodies will always be uniquely different from each other. Don't focus on how unfair it is that another person is losing more weight when you are working just as hard, if not more. Use their progress as inspiration, and just keep working toward your own goals. Inspiration will be a more positive influence than comparison. Accept yourself throughout the process.

17. Words Can Be Inspiring

Have you noticed how motivated you feel when someone reassures you or gives you a good talk? Words have a power of their own. This is why you should consider the power of words in keeping you inspired to lose extra pounds and maintain a healthy weight. We all have a voice in our head that sometimes tells us just to give up, especially when we are doing something that we don't necessarily like or enjoy. Exercising and eating healthy food is not usually as easy as some people make it out to be. It is much easier to eat sugary foods and laze around watching movies. However, you have to ignore the voice telling you to give up and instead listen to the quieter voice that is telling you to keep going.

Whenever you feel a lack of motivation, you should find a way to be inspired. You can ask someone to talk to you and motivate you again. This can be your workout buddy, instructor, family, or just a friend who has seen you work toward your weight loss goals. They will remind you of all your hard work and why you started in the first place. Otherwise, you can just look up some inspirational quotes and keep yourself motivated. Print out some inspirational quotes, and stick them on your desk, locker, wardrobe, gym, or anywhere that will force you to read them. They will be a regular reminder to keep going on your journey.

You can also download a lot of motivational quotes and save them as the wallpaper on your phone or laptop. Seeing these words often will give you more strength. This will prevent you from relapsing into your old habits and destroying the progress you have made. It is actually quite easy to find motivational quotes specifically meant for weight loss. You can also listen to podcasts by people who have gone through the same things as you. Listening to people talk about their journey and how they made progress can help you keep going. Words can be very inspiring when you are feeling completely defeated and on the verge of giving up.

18. Imagine Your Success

Visualize. Imagine yourself achieving the weight loss goals that you have set for yourself. Think of the weighing scale showing the number you want it to. Imagine how you will look in the dress you want to wear to the next party. Visualization can be a powerful tool in your journey. It will show you what you have to look forward to. It will give you a reason to keep going. Imagine succeeding in achieving your goals. Think of the gratification you will experience once you reach that point. The power of visualization is more underrated than it should be. Even before you begin your weight loss plan, you should try visualization.

Get into your mind, and shift the negative mental image that you have of yourself. Don't think of yourself as an overweight and unattractive person because you aren't. However, to motivate yourself to achieve a particular weight loss goal, you can try imagining yourself at that weight. Think of how you will look when you lose the extra pounds and how much happier you will be at that point. Imagine yourself as a fit and successful person. Use this mental image to fuel your persistence in losing weight. This mental trick can be very effective in helping you accept all the hard work that you will have to do along the way. It will make you feel as though all the hard work is worth it, and you will be less willing to give up midway.

Your mind doesn't really know the difference between what you are imagining and what is real. This is why your subconscious will somehow imagine that mental image of yourself as something that has already happened. This kind of visualization has helped many successful people in different fields to build more confidence and attain more success. Studies have shown that this kind of visualization technique has helped many people develop healthy habits and get fit. People who use this trick may even see better results in a shorter time as compared to those who don't try it. You can try this when you wake up in the morning or just before you fall asleep at night. Relax and calm your mind as you picture yourself as you want to be.

Imagine yourself doing all the exercises you should be doing and eating only healthy food. Notice how you feel during all this and try to connect with your emotions. Let this exercise internalize these images. Doing this regularly can be extremely helpful, and you will see how much easier it is for you to follow through with your weight loss plan.

19. Compete with the Past You

If you are aiming for a change in your life, there is always a reason for it. If you are trying to lose weight, you probably have a reason for wanting the change. Most people with weight issues have trouble accepting themselves and face numerous issues associated with excess weight. So, when you are trying to build a new you, compete with the older version of yourself that you were not happy with. Don't repeat the same mistakes that you did before. By now, you should be aware of what you did wrong and how you can do much better.

Motivate yourself to do better than you did before. You are working towards improving yourself, so you cannot afford to be less than what you were before. If you were lazy and avoided physical exercise before, you have to push yourself to be more active. Even if you used to go for a walk, increase your timing compared to before. If you had bad eating habits, work on improving them little by little. Avoid eating sweets or junk food that you used to eat too much off. Don't sit for too long, and avoid binge eating when you are bored or feeling too emotional.

Just try to do better in everything you did before. Think of how much better you will feel about yourself when you see real progress. Everyone can be a better version of themselves at any point in their lives. However, this will require effort and persistence. Don’t fall back on old habits that will make you go through the same unhealthy experience again. In your weight loss journey, you can continuously make an effort to do better than the previous day.

While running, try to increase your pace or your timing a little more than the last time. Add an extra workout day as compared to the previous week. Control your portions a little better than you did before. You will surely see significant progress in your weight loss journey in this way.

There are many ways in which you can challenge yourself or compete with yourself:

- Place a bet. Bet on yourself about something like how much weight you can lose in a certain period of time. You can bet using an app with a friend or just by yourself. It could be money, or it could be a treat you allow yourself if you win the bet. It doesn’t have to be some drastic change or an unhealthy ultimatum. Set a reasonable bet on how much you could easily lose in a couple of weeks. When you win the bet, you will be motivating yourself to keep going and rewarding yourself.

- Make a pact. Make a pact with yourself about doing something different. It could be about going to the gym more regularly than before. Make a pact that you will go to the gym five days a week, no matter what, for two months. Strive to keep this pact with yourself. It could also be about including fresh vegetables in all your meals to eat healthier. Keep a log of these activities to make sure that you stick to your pact.

20. Be Patient

If you are aiming for permanent weight loss, you have to work toward reaching the ideal weight and then maintaining it. Patience is a very important factor in case you want long-term weight loss. If you are not patient, you will probably be making decisions that give you short-term results and leave you disappointed in the long run. Shortsighted decisions are usually associated with diets that are too restrictive; this typically happens when you want to see instant results. This kind of approach will leave you feeling deprived, and at some point, you will resume all your old eating habits.

You might restrict your calories to an unhealthy level, and this can leave you fatigued, nauseous, and feeling ill. This is why you need a dieting approach that will be moderate and give you long-term results. You have to think and plan as you create a weight loss plan that is sustainable for you. Think of the various elements that will give you a sound weight loss plan that ensures success in the long run.

If you stick to your weight loss plan, you will probably be successful in achieving your goals. You have to be patient throughout the process and even after it. Don't assume that your work is done once you lose the extra pounds. Working to maintain this ideal weight can also be quite challenging for most people. You might have expected that the hard part would only have been to lose the weight. You still can't eat as you please and stop exercising altogether. However, you can definitely go a little easier on yourself. Your workouts can be a little less strenuous, and you can allow yourself some unhealthy treats once in a while.

You may even see your weight increase a little sometimes. Don't get anxious or impatient about this. You can easily regain control again. Just be more conscious about what you put on your plate, and don't let your portions be larger than what your body actually needs. People tend to lose patience quite fast, and this applies during the cycle of weight loss. The time it takes to lose the extra pounds off your body will be like a learning period for you. You will understand what your body needs and how it reacts to different things. What you learn in this period will be useful for when you struggle to maintain the new body you have gained. It is not just about what you eat and how much you exercise.

Your attitude toward it all and how you face different challenges play a very important role. Take your time to understand your body, and be patient through it all. Practicing patience will allow you to be successful and motivate you to get back up even when you face a problem. Identify the healthy habits that make you feel good about yourself, and keep repeating them. When something doesn't work out, learn from it, and do something new. Don't let any criticism from other people affect you. Build your confidence, and be patient with yourself. Celebrate your victories, and learn from your failures along the way.

Chapter 6 – 12 Bonus Recipes to Get on with Your Diet

Up to this point, we have seen a lot of tips that can help you to lose weight very effectively. In this chapter, we have included some really easy-to-make and very tasty recipes that will help you with your diet and exercise routines.

Pizza Crust Made of Quinoa

Calories – 90

Carbs – 13 g

Protein – 2 g

Fat – 5 g

Ingredients

- Quinoa, washed and drained, ¾ cup
- Water, ¼ cup
- Salt, ½ teaspoon
- Baking Powder, 1 teaspoon
- Oil, 1 tablespoon (coconut or olive oil recommended)

Method

1. Wash and rinse the quinoa. Let it dry.
2. In a bowl, put in the quinoa, and soak it in some water. Keep it in water for at least 8 hours.

3. When quinoa has been soaked, set the oven on 425 degrees.
4. Rinse the quinoa once again, and then let it dry thoroughly on a towel.
5. In a food processor add the salt, the water, baking powder and finally the quinoa. Process it until you get a thick paste.
6. In a deep baking dish, spread the layer of this paste. You need to oil the pan first.
7. Bake the pizza for 15 minutes, and then turn it over after taking it out.
8. Once again, bake it for around 5 minutes.
9. Take the pizza out, and add your favorite ingredients on top. Bake for around 5 minutes more.
10. Serve hot or cold.

Creamy Thai Soup

Calories – 137

Carbs – 14 g

Protein – 5 g

Fat – 6 g

Ingredients

- Green onions, chopped
- Gluten-free vegetable/chicken stock, 2 cups
- Sun butter, 1 cup
- Garlic, minced, 1 clove
- Ginger, grated or minced, 1-inch piece
- Gluten-free soy sauce, 1 tablespoon
- Honey, 1 teaspoon
- Juice of 1 lime
- Coconut milk, 1 cup
- Red pepper flakes

Method

1. Chop the white part of the green onions. Blend it.
2. Add all the other ingredients and blend until smooth.
3. Cook this blended mixture in a medium-sized pan on medium heat.
4. Serve hot with red pepper flakes.

Green Pea and Parsley Soup

Calories – 210

Carbs – 36 g

Protein – 13 g

Fat – 3 g

Ingredients

- Coconut oil
- Onions, 2 (medium sized)
- Garlic, 4 cloves
- Sea Salt
- Parsley leaves, 2 cups
- Vegetable broth, 3–4 cups
- Lemon juice, 1 tablespoon
- Olive oil, 1 tablespoon
- Peas, ½ kg
- Zest of ½ lemon

Method

1. Chop garlic and onions.
2. In a large pot, heat oil and sauté garlic, onion, salt.
3. Pour in the broth and then the peas. Let it cook. After this, add the parsley. Cook once again. Blend this in a mixer until smooth.
4. Add zest, lemon juice, and oil. Blend this once again.
5. Season with salt, etc., and garnish with parsley.

Stuffed Sweet Potatoes

Calories – 307

Carbs – 53 g

Protein – 15 g

Fat – 5 g

Ingredients

- Sweet potatoes, small, 4
- Olive oil, 1 teaspoon
- Red onion, small, 1
- Garlic, 1 clove
- Cumin powder, 1 teaspoon
- Chilli powder, ½ teaspoon
- Tomatoes, 1 can, chopped
- Black beans, cooked, ½ cup
- Frozen corn kernels, ½ cup
- Chopped cilantro
- Sea salt and ground pepper, to taste

Method

1. Keep oven on preheat mode at 400 F. Bake the sweet potatoes until they are done. Poke them with a fork to get them done faster. You can also microwave them.
2. While the sweet potatoes are getting done, in a medium skillet, soften some onions with olive oil. Next, add garlic, and cook more.

3. To the above mixture, add chili, cumin, and salt and then mix.
4. Add tomatoes, beans, and corn and sauté. Finally, add cilantro, salt, and pepper.
5. When the sweet potatoes are done, take them out of the oven, and slice them down the middle. Season them with salt and pepper, and pour the filling over them.
6. Serve hot.

Baked Paleo Chicken

Calories – 200

Carbs – 0 g

Protein – 41.5 g

Fat – 4.8 g

Ingredients

- Chicken tenderloins, 2 pounds
- Blanched almond flour, 1 cup
- Flax meal, 1 tablespoon
- Paprika, 1 teaspoon
- Garlic powder, ½ teaspoon
- Sea salt, ½ teaspoon
- Dried parsley, ½ teaspoon
- Poultry seasoning, ¼ teaspoon
- Black pepper, ground
- Eggs, 2
- Olive oil spray

Method

1. Keep oven on preheat mode at 425 F, and line two large baking trays with baking paper.
2. In a bowl, add flour, garlic powder, flax meal, paprika sea salt, poultry seasoning, parsley, and pepper.
3. Beat the eggs in a bowl.
4. Coat the chicken with the eggs. Dredge them in the flour mix.

5. Oil the baking sheets, and place the chicken tenders. Bake for 10 minutes, flip spray the oil and bake for another 10 minutes at around 180 F.
6. Serve hot.

Brunch Banana Pancakes

Calories – 78

Carbs – 10 g

Protein – 1.8 g

Fat – 3.5 g

Ingredients

1. Bananas, large and overripe, 2
2. Baking powder, 1/8 teaspoon
3. Eggs, 2
4. Topping of your choice

Method

1. Take a large bowl, and beat eggs with baking powder.
2. Take another bowl, and mash bananas in it.
3. Mix the ingredients of both the bowls in another bowl.
4. Take a frying pan, and make small pancakes. Make at least 10 pancakes with the batter.
5. Serve hot.

Hawaiian Chicken Salad

Calories – 227.3

Carbs – 22 g

Protein – 11 g

Fat – 10.9 g

Ingredients

For the salad

- Shredded cooked chicken, 3 cups
- Chopped green cabbage, 1 cup
- Chopped cilantro/parsley, ¼ cup
- Green onions, finely chopped, ¾ cup
- Fresh chopped pineapple, ½ cup
- Silvered almond, toasted lightly ¼ cup

For the dressing

- Chopped fresh pineapple, ¼ cup
- Lime juice, 1 tablespoon
- Honey, 1 tablespoon
- Fresh ginger root, 1 piece
- Extra virgin olive oil, 1 tablespoon
- Salt
- Black pepper
- Coconut aminos, 2 tablespoons
- Lime zest

Method

1. Blend all the ingredients of the dressing portion in a blender, and blend until it becomes a smooth paste.
2. In a bowl, add all the salad ingredients and toss.
3. Add the dressing to this bowl, and toss once again.
4. Season with salt, pepper, and lime zest.

Vegan Risotto

Calories – 433.5

Carbs – 7.7 g

Protein – 1 g

Fat – 6.9 g

Ingredients

- Olive oil, 1 tablespoon
- Dairy-free margarine, 1 tablespoon
- Garlic, minced, 2 cloves
- White onion, chopped, ¼ cup
- Arborio rice, 2 cups
- Salt
- Ground pepper
- Veggie broth, warm, 6 cups
- White wine, warm, 1 cup
- Zucchini, grated, small, 2
- Diced mushrooms, ½ cup
- Chopped broccoli, 1 cup
- Yeast, 1 tablespoon
- Sun-dried tomatoes, chopped, 2 cups
- Dairy-free margarine, 2 tablespoons
- Basil, chopped, 2 tablespoons

Method

1. In a large pan, heat margarine and oil. Sauté some garlic and onion in it. Add the rice to this pan, and then add the salt and pepper. Let it cook for a bit. Finally add the broth. Let it boil.

2. When the liquid starts reducing, add the wine slowly. Add the vegetables when almost all the wine is used.
3. Remove from heat. Put in margarine, yeast, basil, and tomatoes.
4. Serve hot.

Moo Shu Beef

Calories – 492

Carbs – 48 g

Protein – 34 g

Fat – 18 g

Ingredients

- Top sirloin steak, 1 pound
- Shiitake mushrooms, thinly sliced, ½ cup
- Bean sprouts, ½ cup
- Green cabbage, thinly sliced, 1/2 head
- Carrot, thinly sliced, 1

For the Marinade

- Gluten-free soy sauce, 2 tablespoons
- Dark sesame oil, 1 tablespoon
- Water, 2 tablespoons
- Granulated sugar, 1 tablespoon
- Garlic cloves, minced, 3

For the Sauce

- Gluten-free soy sauce, 2 tablespoons
- Dark sesame oil, 1 tablespoon
- Ground ginger, 1/4 teaspoon
- Granulated sugar, 2 teaspoons
- Water, 2 teaspoons
- Green onion, sliced thinly, 1
- Onion powder, 1/4 teaspoon

- Ground black pepper, 1/2 teaspoon
- Garlic powder, 1/4 teaspoon
- Water, 3 tablespoons
- Cornstarch, 2 teaspoons

Method

1. Take a bowl, and add all ingredients for the marinade. In another bowl, mix all the ingredients for the sauce, except for the cornstarch and water. In another bowl, make slurry of cornstarch and water.
2. Cut the steaks, and marinate them.
3. Heat oil in a skillet, and then cook some steak in it. Now, add the veggies. Let it cook for a bit, and finally, add the slurry.
4. Cook until done.
5. Serve hot over rice.

Amaranth salad

Calories – 251

Carbs – 46 g

Protein – 9.4 g

Fat – 3.9 g

Ingredients

- Cold water, 1 ½ cups
- Uncooked whole-grain amaranth, ½ cup
- Chopped fresh mint, ¼ cup
- Extra-virgin olive oil, 2 tablespoons
- Grated lemon rind, 1 teaspoon
- Pine nuts, toasted, ¼ cup
- Diced unpeeled English cucumber, 2 cups
- Thinly sliced celery, ½ cup
- Chopped fresh flat-leaf parsley, ¼ cup
- Finely chopped red onion, ½ cup
- Fresh lemon juice, 2 tablespoons
- Salt
- Crushed red pepper, ¼ teaspoon
- Canned chickpeas, drained, ½ cup
- Feta cheese, crumbled, 1 cup
- Lemon wedges

Method

1. Boil amaranth in cold water in a sauce pan. Do this on medium heat. Cook until the amaranth absorbs all of the water.

2. Take a bowl, and add everything in it except the cheese and the lemon. Toss.
3. Rinse amaranth under cold running water. Do this in a sieve.
4. In the bowl, add the amaranth and then mix everything together. Serve with lemon wedges and cheese.

Risotto Soup

Calories – 320

Carbs – 46.2 g

Protein – 14.9 g

Fat – 7.5 g

Ingredients

- Olive oil, 1 tablespoon
- Chopped onion, 2 cups
- Grated lemon rind, 2 teaspoons
- Arborio rice, 3/4 cup
- Spinach, coarsely chopped, 2 cups
- Ground nutmeg, ¼ tsp
- Parmesan cheese, grated, ½ cup
- Less-sodium chicken broth, 2 cans
- Asparagus, sliced, 2 cups

Method

1. Take a large sauce pan, and sauté some onions in olive oil. Do this on medium heat. Next, put in the rind and the rice. Sauté once again.
2. Gradually add the broth, and let it simmer. Keep a lid on the pan. Simmer for around 10 minutes.
3. Put in the asparagus and the spinach. Add nutmeg, and cook the broth uncovered.
4. Serve hot when done, and top it with cheese.

Tuna Salad

Calories – 190.3

Carbs – 11.7 g

Protein – 32.3 g

Fat – 2.2 g

Ingredients

- Albacore tuna, 1 can
- Non-fat cottage cheese, 3/4th cup
- Low fat yogurt, 4 tbsp
- Chopped red onion, ¼ cup
- Celery stalk, 1
- Dijon mustard, 1 teaspoon
- Lemon juice
- Dill

Method

1. Take a large salad bowl, and add the tuna in.
2. Then, add the yogurt and cottage cheese, and mix with the tuna.
3. Add the chopped onion and celery.
4. Add a splash of lemon juice, Dijon mustard, and some dill to finish preparing the salad.

Conclusion

Thank you again for choosing this book! I sincerely hope that you received value from it.

I really hope that this book was able to help teach you how to lose weight effectively and permanently. Consistency and constant vigilance are necessary to lose weight and to keep it at bay. It is all about mental strength and power. Losing weight is not important, but losing weight in a healthy way is. You should also try and strive hard to maintain your body.

The next step is to follow the methods listed in this book, and apply what you have just learned. Take action, and be consistent!

Finally, if you enjoyed this book, then I'd like to ask you for a favor, would you be kind enough to leave a review for this audio book? It'd be greatly appreciated! I want to reach as many people as I can with this book and more reviews will help me accomplish that!

Thank you and good luck!

FREE E-BOOKS SENT WEEKLY

Join North Star Readers Book Club
And Get Exclusive Access To The Latest Kindle Books in Health, Fitness, Weight Loss and Much More...

TO GET YOU STARTED HERE IS YOUR FREE E-BOOK:

Visit to Sign Up Today!
www.northstarreaders.com/weight-loss-kick-start

Printed in Great Britain
by Amazon